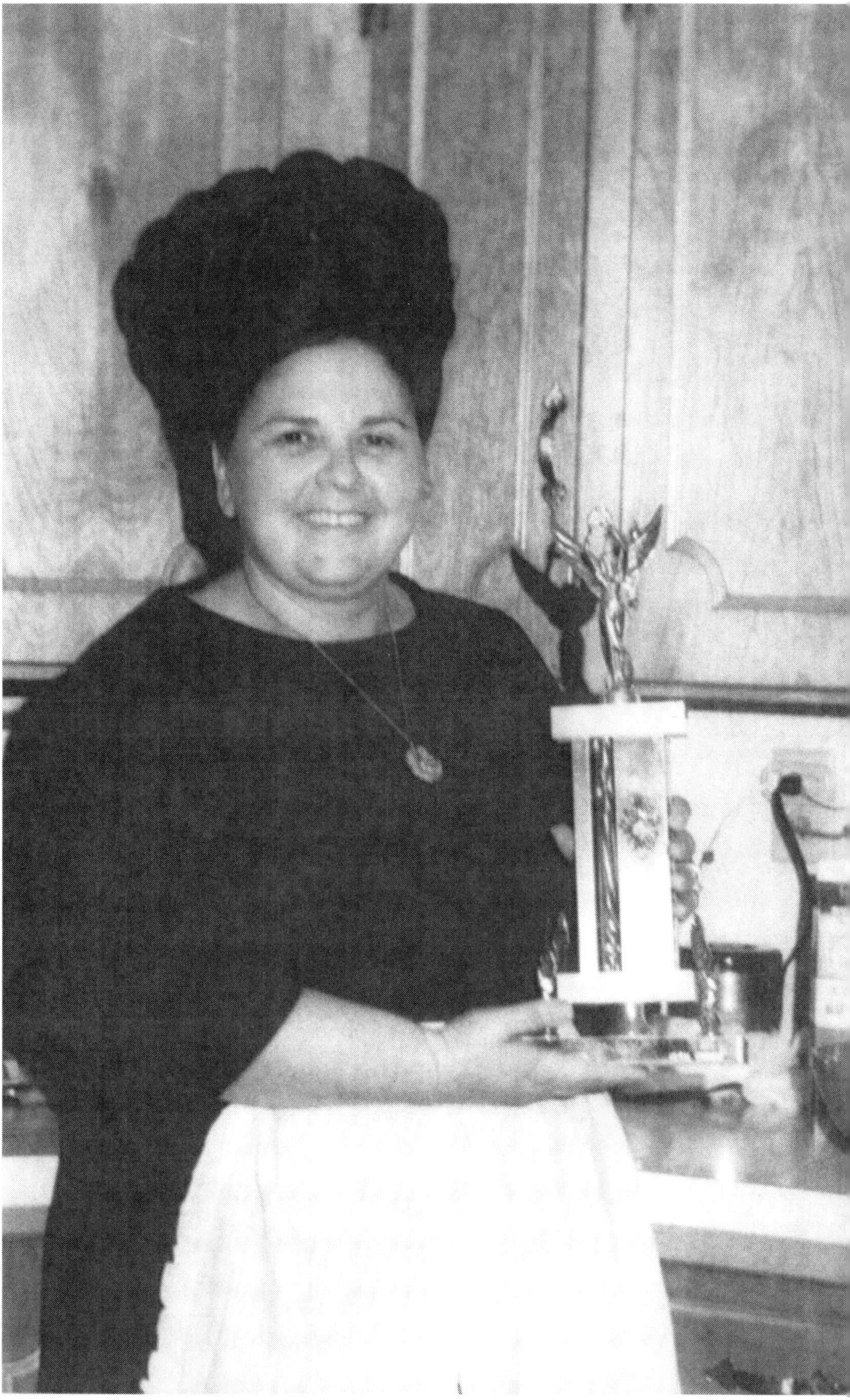

PAGE 110

Aunt Bee's
7 Minute Frosting

3 Egg whites
½ C. White Corn Syrup
1 C Sugar
½ Tsp Cream of tartar

Cook together in top of double boiler on med to High heat, Beat with hand mixer Constantly for seven minutes. Peaks will form, Ready for your Cake.

Vestal

Cooking with Vestal and Friends

SWEET POTATO CASSEROLE
PAGE 35

" This Special Edition has some of Vestal's handwritten recipes, we hope you enjoy them."

© 2004 Goodman Ministries
Manufactured in the United States of America

Even with our busy schedules and everyone going in different directions, we try to have at least one meal together. In our family, the dinner table is where we always seem to meet. And let me tell you, the Goodmans like to eat! I had no choice but to learn how to cook. In my opinion, my mother was the best cook ever, and she was my mentor. We didn't use recipes back then, and a measuring cup, what's that? We had scoops, dashes and a pinch. You added ingredients until it "looked right."

Let me say, we had a time getting these recipes together. When you are compiling a cookbook, you have to have measurements and directions, so we tested each recipe, and when I say tested-well you know! Most of the recipes you will find in this book were handed down for generations in our family, and some came from my friends. Darlin' I hope you have as much fun with this cookbook as we had in making it. If you make one of these recipes and it doesn't turn out just right, do what we used to do, add or take away ingredients until it "looks right." Make your house a "Happy House!"

Love,

Vestal

Contents

APPETIZERS AND DRINKS 7-19
SHRIMP DIP
SPINICH DIP
DRIED BEEF DIP
MARSHMALLOW CRÉME DIP FOR FRUIT
GUACAMOLE DIP
SALSA
PARTY MIX
NACHO LAYERED DIP
TORTILLA ROLLUPS
SLUSH PUNCH
BANANA PUNCH
CHEESE BALL
HOMEMADE SALSA
TEA BASE PUNCH
HAM ROLLS
BLACK BEAN SALSA DIP
YELLOW OR PINK PUNCH
VESTAL'S DEVILED EGGS
SAUSAGE BALLS
CHILI CON QUESO

SALADS AND SOUPS 21-32
CRANBERRY SALAD
MANDARIN ORANGE ALMOND SALAD
SWEET AND SOUR DRESSING
BLUEBERRY SALAD
HOT CHICKEN SALAD
BROCCOLI SALAD
FRUIT SALAD ICE
APRICOT SALAD
FESTIVE FRUIT SALAD
CRANBERRY SALAD
CAULIFLOWER SALAD
APPLE SALAD
WATERGATE SALAD
COLA SALAD
GERMAN POTATO SALAD
MARTHA'S CHICKEN SALAD
CUCUMBER SALAD
LIME PINEAPPLE SALAD
CAESAR DRESSING

VEGETABLES 33-44
CONFETTI CORN
SCALLOPED POTATOES
SWEET POTATO CASSEROLE
BETTY'S CREAM SPINACH WITH VESTAL'S TOUCH
SQUASH CASSEROLE
POTATOES ROMANOFF
CARROTS A L'ORANGE
GREEN BEAN CASSEROLE
SQUASH CASSEROLE
BROCCOLI CASSEROLE
BAKED BEANS CASSEROLE
POT LUCK POTATO CASSEROLE
FATTENIN' MASHED POTATOES
SPANISH CORN
BROCCOLI AND RICE CASSEROLE
CREAMED CORN
SHERRY'S JALAPENO CORN
RENEE'S CORN AU GRATIN
EGGPLANT PARMESAN
BAKED BEANS

BREADS 45-54
BANANA NUT BREAD
OATMEAL 'N' RAISIN MUFFINS
ZUCCHINI BREAD
FRENCH BREAKFAST MUFFINS
ANGEL ROLLS
MAMAW McKINNEY'S HOT ROLLS
CRANBERRY ORANGE BREAD
BLUEBERRY MUFFINS
SQUASH SPOON BREAD
BUTTERMILK BISCUITS
PUMPKIN BREAD
FAYE'S PANCAKES
CORNBREAD
BLUEBERRY PANCAKES
ONE HOUR ROLLS
VESTAL'S FAMOUS SPOON BISCUITS (CATHEAD BISCUITS)
VESTAL'S COUNTRY GRAVY

CASSEROLE 55-70
HOLIDAY DRESSING
BAKED GRITS
CHICKEN CASSEROLE
HOT TAMALE CASSEROLE
CREAMY CHICKEN ENCHILADAS
CHICKEN SPAGHETTI
MACARONI AND CHEESE

CHICKEN POT PIE
MEMAW'S MEATLOAF
CHICKEN CASSEROLE
CHILI RELLENO CASSEROLE
OVEN STEW
BREAKFAST SAUSAGE CASSEROLE
LASAGNA
CAVATINI
CHICKEN VEGETABLE CASSEROLE
CHICKEN DIVAN
CHICKEN ENCHILADAS
PARTY EGGS
MEDIUM WHITE CREAM SAUCE
CHICKEN BREASTS IN SOUR CREAM GRAVY
BACON WRAPPED CHICKEN BREAST
SWEET AND SOUR CHICKEN
AUNTIE'S THICK SLAB BACON
GIBLET GRAVY

MAIN DISHES 71-86
CHICKEN DIJON
BARBECUED HAMBURGERS
CHICKEN & DUMPLINGS
SLOPPY JOE'S
OVEN FRIED CHICKEN
CRUSTLESS QUICHE
MEXICAN QUICHE
FANCY EGG SCRAMBLE
CHEESE SAUCE
CRUST FOR QUICHE
HAMBURGER STROGANOFF
SALMON PATTIES
FAYE'S PORK CHOPS
CRANBERRY CHICKEN
SEAFOOD FOR 10
CLASSIC SPAGHETTI AND MEATBALLS
VEGETABLE BEEF STEW
NEW ORLEANS STYLE BARBECUE SHRIMP
SWEET AND SOUR PORK
SWEET AND SOUR RICE
STEAK AND RICE
CREOLE SHRIMP
OVEN BARBECUED CHICKEN
FETTUCCINI ALFREDO

PHOTO ALBUM OF FAMILY AND FRIENDS 87-98

DESSERTS 99-141
VESTAL'S TOFFEE
DUMP CAKE

BREAD PUDDING
CHOCOLATE PECAN PIE
CHOCOLATE FUDGE
LEMON CAKE
MOLASSES COOKIES
CHRISTMAS DONUTS
BANANA PUDDING
PUMPKIN PIE
JAM CAKE
PECAN PIE
FRUIT COCKTAIL CAKE
DOUBLE CHOCOLATE FANTASY BARS
COOKIE FROSTING
DATE BARS
STRAWBERRY DELIGHT
COCONUT KISSES
TURTLE PIE
7 MINUTE FROSTING
GRAHAM CRACKER CAKE
CREAMY RICE PUDDING
AUNT BEA'S FRUIT CAKE
RICH LEMON BARS
ARKANSAS DIRT
FRESH APPLE CAKE
PUMPKIN ICE CREAM PIE
CHESS PIE
MANDARIN ORANGE FLUFF CAKE
BOBBIE'S DUMP CAKE
AUNT BEA'S QUICK FRUIT PIE
DERBY PIE
THANKSGIVING & CHRISTMAS CHOCOLATE PIE
CHOCOLATE SOUFFLÉ
CUSTARD SAUCE
POUND CAKE
IRON SKILLET CHOCOLATE PIE
RASPBERRY CHANTILLY
CHOCAROON CAKE
CHESS CAKE
MINT DAZZLE DESSERT
WINTER FRUIT COMPOTE
FRESH PEACH PIE
BUTTER CRUST
SNOW PUDDING
LOIS' LEMON SUPREME SPECIAL
TEXAS SHEET CAKE
LEMON CAKE
$300 STRAWBERRY CAKE
GRANNY'S TEA CAKES
MICROWAVE CHOCOLATE PIE
SWEDISH PECAN BALLS

BUCK EYES
COLD BREAD PUDDING
PUDDING DIP
CRISP OATMEAL COOKIES
OLD FASHIONED BUTTERMILK PIE
CHOCOLATE SYRUP BROWNIES
SNOW ICE CREAM
SOUR CREAM POUNDCAKE
DOUBLE GOOD BROWNIES
PEANUT BRITTLE
GRAPE ICE CREAM
MAGIC COOKIES
APPLE STRUDEL
PINEAPPLE UPSIDE DOWN CAKE
COCONUT PIE
JAPANESE CHOCOLATE PIE
FRESH COCONUT CAKE
CHOCOLATE PIE
TREASURE COOKIES
SOCK IT TO ME CAKE
GLAZE FOR SOCK IT TO ME CAKE
BRITTNEY COOKIES
CHOCOLATE GRAVY
CHERRY CHEESE PIE
CHOCOLATE COVERED BALLS

SPECIAL FRIENDS 143-157
GEORGE JONES' SPICY THREE BEAN SOUP
JANET PASCHAL'S LEMON PIE
NEVER FAIL MERINGUE
GLORIA GAITHER'S WHEAT BREAD
NEWSBOYS AUSTRALIAN SUNDAY LUNCH ROASTED LEG OF LAMB
VINCE GILL'S FAVORITE RECIPE
KATINA'S FRUIT PIZZA
ISLANDS IN THE STREAM BY DOLLY PARTON
JAKE HESS' ORANGE JELL-O SALAD
RUSS TAFF'S CHILI DOGS
SANDI PATTY'S MOST SPECTACULAR MEATLOAF
ANDRAE CROUCH'S FRIED CHICKEN
CARMAN'S FAVORITE SPAGHETTI SAUCE AND MEATBALLS

Appetizers & Drinks

SHRIMP DIP

2 large triangles Hoop cheese
1 1/2 pints mayonnaise
8 oz. cream cheese
1 large white onion
1 clove garlic
6-8 large jalepeno peppers seedless and chopped
2 lb. boiled shrimp

Grate Hoop cheese through small holes in grater, into large mixing bowl. Add mayonnaise and mix until fluffy. Add cream cheese, which has been chopped up. Put onion in blender and chop finely. Add onion and garlic to cheese mixture. This makes a large bowl full. After it is well blended, add jalepeno peppers and shrimp and mix with hands. Chill and serve with crackers.

SPINICH DIP

10 oz. package frozen chopped spinach
1/2 teaspoon pepper
1/2 teaspoon garlic powder
1 pint mayonnaise
1 teaspoon salt
1/2 cup chopped onion
parsley flakes
juice of 1 lemon

Thaw spinach, drain. Put all ingredients in blender and blend well. Chill and serve with crackers, chips or raw vegetables.

DRIED BEEF DIP

16 oz. cream cheese
1 jar dried beef, finely chopped
1 can cream of mushroom soup
1/4 cup catsup
1 small onion

In a bowl, soften cream cheese. Add dried beef along with remaining ingredients to cheese mixture and blend well. Chill and serve with chips or crackers.

MARSHMALLOW CRÉME DIP FOR FRUIT

1 cup powdered sugar
8 oz. cream cheese
7 oz. marshmallow cream
dash of orange peel for garnish

Mix first 3 ingredients together well and garnish with orange peel. Serve with strawberries, apples, pineapple, grapes, pears or whatever you like.

GUACAMOLE DIP

6 avocados, cut up
1 medium onion, finely chopped
1-2 green chili peppers, finely chopped
2 tablespoon lemon juice
1 1/2 teaspoon salt
1/2 teaspoon black pepper
1 tablespoon fruit fresh
1 medium tomato

Beat avocados, onion, peppers, lemon juice, salt, pepper and fruit fresh until creamy. Stir in tomato. Cover and refrigerate for at least 1 hour. Serve with warm tortilla chips.

SALSA

1 can Mexican stewed tomatoes
1/2 cup finely chopped onion
2 tablespoon chopped fresh cilantro
2 teaspoon lemon juice
1 small clove garlic, minced
1/8 teaspoon hot pepper sauce

Place tomatoes in blender container, cover and run on lowest speed 2 seconds to chop tomatoes. Combine with onion, cilantro, lemon juice, garlic and pepper sauce. Add additional pepper sauce if desired. Serve with warm tortilla chips.

PARTY MIX

1 large box sweetened oat cereal
1 large box donut shaped cereal
1 large box wheat, rice or corn Chex cereal
1 box stick pretzels
2 lbs pecan halves
1 bottle Worcestershire sauce
4 tablespoon seasoned salt
4 tablespoon celery salt
4 tablespoon chili powder
2 teaspoon hot pepper sauce
4 tablespoon garlic powder
1 lb margarine
2 cups bacon fat
2 tablespoon liquid smoke

Mix cereals, pretzels and pecans in a large roasting pan. Combine remaining ingredients and bring to a boil in a saucepan. Pour over dry mixture, spreading evenly and mixing well. Put in preheated 200° oven and stir every 10 minutes. After about 1 1/2 hours, check to see if dry mixture has soaked up all of the juice or is almost dry. Let cool and store in tins. You can substitute pecans for peanuts if you choose. This is great for the holidays.

NACHO LAYERED DIP

2 cans bean dip
1 pint sour cream
1 package taco seasoning
2 chopped avocados
1 tablespoon lemon juice
3 chopped tomatoes
1 can chopped green chilies
1 bunch chopped green onions
1/4 cup chopped black olives
1/4 lb grated cheddar cheese

Mix taco seasoning with sour cream. Mix lemon juice with avocados. Layer in order given in a shallow dish. Serve with warm tortilla chips.

TORTILLA ROLLUPS

1 small jar drained jalepeno peppers, medium to hot
8 oz. cream cheese
1 package Hidden Valley Ranch powder
1/2 lb shaved roast beef or ham
1 cup grated cheese
1 package flour tortillas
1 16 oz. carton sour cream

Soften cream cheese and mix with sour cream, ranch dressing powder. Spread thick layer completely over tortilla. Place roast beef or ham on top. Sprinkle grated cheese over and roll up tightly. Seal with plastic wrap or foil. Let set in refrigerator until ready to serve. Slice into pinwheels and serve with salsa.

SLUSH PUNCH

2 boxes flavored gelatin
1 cup sugar

Use water as directed for gelatin and mix the above and set aside.

2 cans frozen lemonade
2 cans frozen orange juice
water as directed on cans
1 can unsweetened pineapple juice

Mix all ingredients with gelatin mixture and freeze. When ready to use, let thaw a couple of hours. Before using, add chilled ginger ale to your taste.

BANANA PUNCH

1 can pineapple juice
1 can frozen orange juice concentrate made as directed
6 cups water
4 cups sugar
juice of 2 lemons
5 bananas

Heat water and sugar until dissolved. Mix all the remaining ingredients together with sugar and water mixture. Cool and then freeze. When ready to serve, set out of freezer 3 hours before serving, until it is mushy. Put in punch bowl and pour 3 quarts of ginger ale over mixture.

CHEESE BALL

1 lb Velveeta cheese
8 oz. cream cheese
1 jar Old English cheese spread
add garlic to taste
1 tablespoon Worcestershire sauce
4 drops Tabasco sauce
1 1/2 cups pecans

Place sliced jalepenos on top of meat. Soften cheese to room temperature before combining ingredients. Combine all ingredients reserving 1/2 cup of pecans. Chill and form into 2 balls. Sprinkle tops with reserved pecans.

HOMEMADE SALSA

1 large can whole tomatoes
3 cloves garlic
2 green onions
1 1/2 tablespoon cilantro
1/2 lemon
dash of oregano
dash of salt
dash of crushed cumin

Chop all ingredients and stir together in a bowl. Squeeze the juice of 1/2 lemon into salsa. Add dash of oregano, crushed cumin and salt to taste. For best results, refrigerate overnight. Serve with warm tortilla chips.

TEA BASE PUNCH

4 tea bags
2 cups boiling water
3 large lemons
2 cups sugar
4 cups cold water
1 teaspoon vanilla
1 teaspoon almond extract
2 quarts ginger ale

Pour boiling water over tea bags, cover and steep for 10 minutes. Set aside. Wash lemons and extract juice. Add the lemon rinds to cold water and sugar. Bring to a boil. Remove from heat and add juice and tea. Cool and add extracts. Mix well and add ginger ale. Serve over ice in punch bowl.

HAM ROLLS
(1) 10oz. refrigerated pizza crust
2 tablespoon plain nonfat yogurt
2 teaspoon Dijon mustard
1 teaspoon drained white horseradish
6oz. thinly sliced broiled ham
3oz. shredded cheddar cheese
1/2 cup diced onion

On work surface, stretch pizza dough into 12 x 10 inch rectangle. In small bowl, whisk together yogurt, mustard and horseradish. Spread mixture evenly over dough, leaving 1 1/2 inch border. Arrange ham over dough, sprinkle with cheese and onion. Starting from wide end, roll dough in a jellyroll fashion to enclose filling. Pinch seam to seal. Spray non-stick cooking spray. Arrange roll seam side down on cookie sheet. Bake 15 minutes in a 425° oven, until golden brown. Let cool 10 minutes before cutting into 10 equal slices.

BLACK BEAN SALSA DIP
2 cans black beans
1 medium onion finely chopped
1 small green pepper, chopped
2 cloves garlic, minced
1 tablespoon oil
1 cup salsa
2 teaspoon cumin
1/2 teaspoon salt
1/4 cup chopped cilantro
1 cup shredded cheddar cheese

(continued on next page)

1/2 cup chopped tomatoes
1/2-1 cup sour cream, as desired

Rinse and drain one can of beans. Place un-drained contents of remaining can of beans in blender or food processor and blend until smooth. In 10 inch skillet, cook onion, green pepper and garlic in oil until onion is tender, but not brown. Add whole and pureed beans, salsa, cumin and salt, mix well and bring to a boil. Reduce heat and simmer uncovered, stirring occasionally 12-15 minutes or until thickened. Stir in cilantro and transfer dip to shallow serving dish and sprinkle with cheese. Serve with warm chips or vegetables. Makes 6-8 servings.

YELLOW OR PINK PUNCH
1 large can pineapple juice
2 cups boiling water
2 packages lemon or strawberry Jell-O
6 cups cold water
1 cup sugar
1 can frozen orange juice
1 can frozen lemonade
1 quart ginger ale
1/2 gallon vanilla ice cream

Add boiling water to Jell-O, stir until dissolved. Dissolve sugar with Jell-O. Add cold water and juices. Add ginger ale and ice cream just before serving. Garnish punch bowl with slices of lemon or oranges.

VESTAL'S DEVILED EGGS

6 hard boiled eggs, cooled and peeled
3 tablespoon mayonnaise
1 teaspoon mustard
1/3 teaspoon black pepper
pinch of salt
2 teaspoon sweet pickle relish
paprika to taste

Slice eggs in half and remove yolks. Place yolks in large mixing bowl and use a fork to mash into a paste. Add remaining ingredients and mix well. Put yolk mixture into egg whites and sprinkle with paprika and serve.

SAUSAGE BALLS

3 cups buttermilk biscuit mix
1 lb grated cheddar cheese
1 lb sausage (raw)

Mix all ingredients. Form into balls and bake on cookie sheet for 20-22 minutes at 325°.

CHILI CON QUESO

1 box Velveeta cheese
2 cans Rotel tomatoes and green chilies
2 sticks butter
(1) 2 1/2 lb box Velveeta
2 tabelspoons self rising flour
1 large can evaporated milk or 2 cups homogenized milk
2 heaping tablespoons chopped pimentos (optional)

In large heavy saucepan, melt butter. Add flour, stir and cook until flour lightly browns. Stir constantly. Turn heat lower and add both cans of tomatoes and chilies, mix well. Add canned milk or regular milk and pimentos. Cook for 3-5 minutes on low heat. Cut cheese in large slices and add slowly. Stir until cheese is melted. Continue to stir. Turn heat to simmer, eat with chips. This can be stored in refrigerator and reheated in single servings.

Salads & Soups

CRANBERRY SALAD

2 cups cranberries, ground
3/4 cup sugar
1/2 cup seedless grapes
1/4 teaspoon salt
2 cups miniature marshmallows
2 cups unpared apples
1/2 cup chopped walnuts
1 cup whipping cream

Combine cranberries, marshmallows and sugar, cover and chill overnight. When ready to serve, add apples, grapes, walnuts and salt, then fold in whipping cream.

MANDARIN ORANGE ALMOND SALAD

1 head of green leaf lettuce
1 sliced red onion
1 can mandarin oranges, drained
1/2 cup sliced almonds, toasted and sugared *

Combine in large salad bowl. *For every 1/2 cup of almonds, use about 4 1/2 tablespoons of sugar. Cook over a very low heat stirring constantly, until sugar is liquid and covers all of the almonds. This takes a while. Cut lettuce for salad. Combine all ingredients and top with toasted almonds. Toss with sweet and sour dressing.

(Recipe for dressing on page 23)

SWEET AND SOUR DRESSING

1/4 cup vegetable oil
2 tablespoon sugar
2 tablespoon vinegar
1 tablespoon parsley
1/2 teaspoon salt
4-5 dashes of Tabasco sauce
dash of pepper
dash of salt

Combine all ingredients and place over salad just before you are ready to serve.

BLUEBERRY SALAD

2 3oz. packages black cherry Jell-O
2 cups boiling water
(1) 8 1/4 oz. can crushed pineapple, drained
(1) 16 oz. can blueberries, partially drained

Add hot water to Jell-O and completely dissolve. Add pineapple and blueberries. Place in 2 quart Jell-O mold and set.

TOPPING:
8 oz. cream cheese
1/2 cup sour cream
1/2 cup sugar
1/2 cup nuts

Cream together cream cheese, sour cream and sugar. Spread over Jell-O and sprinkle with nuts.

HOT CHICKEN SALAD

3 cups cooked diced chicken
3/4 cup sliced almonds
1 can sliced water chestnuts
1 can cream of chicken soup
2 teaspoon minced onion
1 1/2 cups diced celery
1 1/2 cups mayonnaise
salt to taste

Place all ingredients in 9 x 12 inch pan or dish.

TOPPING:
1 1/2 cups crushed potato chips
3/4 cup grated cheddar cheese

Top casserole with topping and bake at 325 degrees until brown. May be frozen and heated later.

BROCCOLI SALAD

1 cup mayonnaise
1/4 cup sugar
2 tablespoon apple cider vinegar

Mix and refrigerate overnight.

TOSS WITH:
1 bunch broccoli flowerets, chopped, no stems
1/2 cup chopped vidalia onion
1/3 cup raisins
1/3 cup bacon bits

FRUIT SALAD ICE

1 large package frozen strawberries
1 large can crushed pineapple
1 large can apricots, drained
4 diced bananas
1 cup water
1 1/4 cups sugar

Combine fruits. Cook sugar and water to make syrup. Pour over fruit while hot. Line Muffin pan with cupcake liners. Pour fruit mixture into cupcake liners. Freeze until solid. Take salads out of tins and store in freezer bags. Take papers off when ready to serve. Serve on a lettuce leaf. Makes 20-30. Use half recipe for 12-14.

APRICOT SALAD

1 8oz. package dried apricots
1 1/2 teaspoon lemon juice
1 1/2 cups half & half
1 4oz. package cream cheese
3 envelopes unflavored gelatin
1 1/2 cups whipping cream
4 1/2 teaspoon sugar
1 large can apricot halves, drained

Place dried apricots in small pan and rinse with cold water. Drain and cover with warm water and simmer 15 minutes until soft, adding more water if necessary. Place apricots and liquid, 3 tablespoons sugar and lemon juice in blender and puree. Pour into medium sized mixing bowl, let stand until cool. Add half-and-half and mix well. Place gelatin in small heavy saucepan and add 6 tablespoons of water to soften. Let stand for 5 minutes. Place over low heat and stir until dissolved. Stir into apricot mixture. Whip cream until stiff. After apricot mixture has cooled, fold in whipped cream. Pour into oiled salad mold and chill until set. Mix cream cheese and remaining sugar until smooth. Fill 8 halves of apricots with cream cheese mixture. Top with the other halves. Pipe cream cheese around the center to hold them together. Use as a garnish for the molded salad.

FESTIVE FRUIT SALAD

1 can peach pie filling
1 can pineapple chunks, drained
2-3 bananas
1 can mandarin oranges, drained
(2) 10 oz. packages frozen strawberries with syrup, thawed

Mix all ingredients adding bananas just before serving.

CRANBERRY SALAD

1 lb. raw cranberries
finely ground

Measure ground cranberries and cover with an equal amount of sugar. Let stand several hours, then drain and add;

1/2 cup celery, chopped
1/2 cup nuts, chopped
1 cup small marshmallows
1/2 pint sweetened whipping cream, whipped
1/2 cup purple seedless grapes

Mix well and serve chilled.

CAULIFLOWER SALAD

1 head of cauliflower
1 small can ripe olives
3-4 green onions
1 teaspoon sugar
1/2 cup mayonnaise
1/2 cup salad dressing
dash of salt and pepper

Separate cauliflower in flowerets. Slice thinly crosswise. Slice black olives crosswise also. Chop onion finely. Mix together salad dressing, mayonnaise, sugar, salt and pepper and toss together.

APPLE SALAD

1 can fruit cocktail
1 can crushed pineapple, drained, reserve juice
3 cups small marshmallows
5 apples, chopped

Mix together and set aside.

3 tablespoon flour
1 cup sugar
2 eggs
2 teaspoon mustard
juice of 1 lemon
pineapple juice

Mix flour and sugar. Beat eggs well and add mustard, lemon juice and pineapple juice and mix again. Add to sugar and (continued on next page)

flour mixture and mix. Cook over medium heat until thick. Cool. Pour over fruit salad and mix.
Toss with following ingredients;

1 can coconut
1 lb. grated American or cheddar cheese

WATERGATE SALAD
1 carton Cool Whip
1 small package pistachio pudding mix
1 can crushed pineapple
1/2 cup slivered almonds
maraschino cherries

Combine all ingredients. Garnish top with cherries or almonds.

COLA SALAD
1 can bing cherries
1 can crushed pineapple
2 packages cherry Jell-O
2 cups cola
1 package cream cheese
1 cup chopped nuts

Drain juice from cherries and pineapple. Heat and pour on flavored gelatin to dissolve. Cool. Add cola. Halve bing cherries and remove stones. Chop up cream cheese. Add these and other ingredients to the flavored gelatin when it has thickened slightly. Chill.

GERMAN POTATO SALAD

8 medium red new potatoes
1 large bottle Hidden Valley Ranch dressing
1 jar bacon bits
1 bunch green onions

Cook potatoes, leaving skin on, cool and dice, chop onion and add all ingredients. Salt and pepper to taste.

MARTHA'S CHICKEN SALAD

3 cups cooked and diced chicken
1 cup diced celery
1 cup mandarin orange sections
1 can pineapple tidbits
2 tablespoon salad oil
2 tablespoon orange juice
2 tablespoon vinegar
1/2 teaspoon salt
dash of marjoram
1/2 cup mayonnaise or salad dressing
1/2 cup slivered almonds, toasted

Combine chicken, celery, oranges and pineapple. Blend salad oil, orange juice, vinegar, salt and marjoram. Add chicken mixture, chill for one hour. Drain. Add mayonnaise and toss. Sprinkle almonds on top. Serve immediately.

CUCUMBER SALAD

1/2 cup diced cucumbers
1/2 cup diced onions
1/2 cup diced tomatoes
1/4 teaspoon seasoned salt
1/2 teaspoon black pepper
1/4 teaspoon paprika
1/2 cup sour cream

Mix well and chill. Wonderful served with dinner.

LIME PINEAPPLE SALAD

1 large package lime Jell-O
1 large can crushed pineapple
1 cup evaporated milk
8oz. cottage cheese
2 tablespoon sugar
1 cup chopped pecans
1/2 teaspoon salt
1/2 cup mayonnaise

Drain pineapple in measuring cup and add enough water to pineapple juice to equal a cup. Heat to a boil and add Jell-O stirring to dissolve. Set aside to cool. In large bowl, pour drained pineapple, milk, sugar, salt, cottage cheese, mayonnaise and chopped pecans. Stir until mixed well. Add Jell-O mixture to pineapple mixture and stir well. Pour into gelatin mold that has been sprayed with cooking oil. Refrigerate until congealed. Turn out on lettuce leaf, garnish with cherries and pecan halves.

CAESAR DRESSING

3 egg yolks
1/2 tube anchovy paste
1 pint salad oil
1/3 cup minced garlic
1 pint olive oil
3/8 cup lemon juice
1/4 cup Worchestershire sauce
1/4 cup Dijon mustard
4 tablespoon Tabasco sauce
3/4 tablespoon parmesan cheese
1/2 cup tarragon vinegar

Whip eggs on high speed and add oils and mix on slow speed with rest of ingredients. Salt and pepper to taste.

Vegetables

CONFETTI CORN

1 can creamed corn
2/3 cup bread crumbs
dash black pepper
1/2 cup milk
2 tablespoon chopped onion
2 tablespoon green pepper
2 tablespoon pimentos
2 tablespoon butter

Mix all ingredients. Pour into oiled casserole dish. Bake at 350° for 35 to 40 minutes.

SCALLOPED POTATOES

1 cup shredded sharp cheese
6 medium potatoes
1 medium onion
1 can cream of mushroom soup
garlic salt to taste

Peel potatoes and cut into thick potato chips. Grease the casserole pan with shortening. Place potatoes into pan and set aside. In saucepan, place chopped onion, soup, cheese and two good shakes of garlic salt. Heat at low temperature until soupy. Pour over potatoes. Cook at 350° for 25 minutes or until the potatoes are tender when pierced with a fork. This same cheese sauce may be used on asparagus, broccoli, or 1 cup minute rice mixed with 1 can of tuna.

SWEET POTATO CASSEROLE

1 large can yams
1 cup coconut
1 stick butter
1/2 cup milk
1 teaspoon vanilla
2 beaten eggs
1 cup sugar

Mix together with mixer and place in 13 x 9 inch Pyrex.

TOPPING:
1/2 cup flour
1 cup brown sugar
1 cup chopped pecans
1 stick melted butter

Mix flour and sugar in bowl and add 2 tablespoons of hot water, butter and the pecans. Spoon on top of yam mixture. Bake 30-45 minutes at 350° until golden brown.

BETTY'S CREAM SPINACH WITH VESTAL'S TOUCH

2 packages frozen chopped spinach
1 medium onion, finely chopped
1 teaspoon chopped garlic
1/2 teaspoon Lawry's seasoning salt
1/4 teaspoon white pepper
3-4 strips bacon chopped
1/2 stick butter
2 tablespoon flour
1 1/2 cups milk
1/4 cup grated parmesan cheese

Sauté bacon in heavy saucepan until almost brown. Add onion and garlic, cook until onions are clear. Add butter and flour, cook until flour is tan and add salt and milk, stirring well. Now add drained spinach and mix. Pour into greased casserole dish. Sprinkle with cheese. Cook 15 minutes or until cheese is brown in a 400 degree oven. I ain't telling what I added, but 'tis delicious.

SQUASH CASSEROLE

10-15 medium sized squash
5 eggs
3 cups milk
1/2 cup butter
1/4 cup melted butter
1/2 teaspoon pepper
1/2 cup dry onions
bread crumbs

Boil squash, drain and place in a loaf pan. Mix butter, milk and eggs with squash. Sprinkle with bread crumbs and 1/4 cup melted butter. Bake for 20-25 minutes at 350°.

POTATOES ROMANOFF
5 packages frozen potato patties
3 cups shredded cheddar cheese
2 teaspoon salt
1/2 teaspoon dry mustard
2 pints sour cream
1 bunch green onions
1/2 teaspoon pepper

Thaw potato patties in microwave or at room temperature until almost thawed, still icy. Combine all ingredients in large bowl. Pour into oiled or sprayed baking pan. Top with additional grated cheese. Bake at 350° for 30-40 minutes.

CARROTS A L'ORANGE
1 1/2 lbs. carrots, sliced thin, peeled
1 1/2 tablespoon orange marmalade
1 tablespoon margarine
dash nutmeg

Cook carrots in 1 inch boiling water in covered pan until almost tender. Drain well, add marmalade, margarine and nutmeg and glaze over medium heat, shaking pan frequently.

GREEN BEAN CASSEROLE

3 cans whole green beans
garlic salt to taste
(1) 8 oz. sour cream
1 can mushroom soup
8 oz. pasteurized process cheese
round butter crackers

Heat green beans in their juice. When hot, drain. Mix with salt, sour cream and soup. Put into 3 quart casserole dish and put cheese over top. Top cheese with crushed crackers. Bake 350° about 30 minutes.

SQUASH CASSEROLE

2 packages frozen squash
1 large onion, chopped
3 tablespoon margarine
2 cans cream of mushroom soup
(1) 8 oz.. carton of sour cream
salt and pepper
1 package season stuffing mix
1 cup shredded sharp cheddar cheese

Cook squash until tender. Sauté squash and onion in margarine. Mix soup, sour cream, salt and pepper to taste and set aside. Line a 2-3 quart casserole with a layer of stuffing, layer of squash and layer of soup mixture. Top with cheese and bake at 350° for 30 minutes until bubbly.

BROCCOLI CASSEROLE

2 packages chopped broccoli, cooked
1/2 cup butter
6 teaspoon flour
6 eggs
4 cups cottage cheese
8 oz. pasteurized process cheese, cubed

Cook broccoli according to package directions, drain. Melt butter, stir flour into butter. Beat eggs and add to flour and butter mixture a little bit at a time. Add remaining ingredients and stir well. Bake in glass casserole dish, uncovered at 350° for 30-45 minutes.

BAKED BEANS CASSEROLE

1 lb ground beef
2 medium onions, chopped
1 medium bell pepper, chopped
1 garlic button
1 1/2 bottles catsup
salt and pepper to taste
2 tablespoon brown sugar
1 tablespoon dry mustard
2 cans pork and beans

Brown meat, onion and bell pepper slowly in small amount of shortening in skillet. When browned, add garlic, catsup, brown sugar, salt and pepper and mustard. Let simmer for about 1 1/2 hours or until it thickens a little. Then add beans and simmer for 30 minutes uncovered.

POT LUCK POTATO CASSEROLE

1 large package frozen hashbrowns
1 can cream of chicken soup
1/2 cup finely chopped onion
1 cup sour cream
1/2 teaspoon parsley
1/2 cup milk
2 cups grated cheddar cheese
1/2 cup melted margarine
1 teaspoon salt
1/2 teaspoon pepper
2 cups crushed corn flakes

Combine all ingredients in large bowl, except the 1/2 cup of margarine and the corn flakes. Pour into buttered Pyrex 9 x 13. Cover top with crushed corn flakes, pour over 1/2 cup margarine. Bake 45 minutes at 350°. Great dish to take to a party!

FATTENIN' MASHED POTATOES

9 large potatoes, peeled and cooked
1/2 teaspoon salt
2 tablespoon butter
8 oz. sour cream
6 oz. cream cheese
2 teaspoon onion salt

Mash potatoes and add all ingredients. Bake in 9 x 13 Pyrex at 350° for 30 minutes or until heated through.

SPANISH CORN

1 can cream style corn
1 cup Bisquick
1 egg
2 tablespoon melted butter
1/2 cup milk
1 can chopped jalapeno
1 cup grated Monterey Jack cheese

Combine corn, Bisquick, eggs, butter and milk. Pour 1/2 into greased 2 quart baking dish. Sprinkle with chopped peppers and cheese. Add remaining ingredients and mix well. Bake at 350° for 30-45 minutes

BROCCOLI AND RICE CASSEROLE

1 cup minute rice
1 cup cold water
1/2 cup chopped celery
8 oz. jar cheese whiz
1/2 cup chopped onion
2/3 stick margarine
10 1/2 oz. chopped broccoli
1 can cream of mushroom soup

Heat soup, water, cheese and margarine over low heat until margarine and cheese melts. Remove from heat and mix other ingredients. Pour into greased casserole dish and bake 1 hour at 300°.

CREAMED CORN

2 cans shoe peg whole kernel corn, drained
1 stick melted butter
2 tablespoon flour
1/2 pint whipping cream

Place corn in baking dish. Mix remaining ingredients and pour over corn. Bake for 30 minutes at 350°.

SHERRY'S JALAPENO CORN

1 stick of butter
6 oz. cream cheese
1/8 cup milk
garlic powder to taste
2 cans of white shoepeg corn, drained
1 1/2 jalapenos

Melt butter, cream cheese, milk and garlic together over low heat. Add corn and jalapeno.

RENEE'S CORN AU GRATIN

1 lb frozen whole kernel corn
16 oz. whipping cream
1 1/2 tablespoon butter
1/2 teaspoon salt
1/2 teaspoon accent
1 1/2 tablespoon flour
3 tablespoon sugar
3 tablespoon Parmesan cheese

Put corn and cream in pot and bring to a boil. Simmer 5 minutes and season with salt, sugar and accent. Make paste with butter and flour, add to cream corn mixture as thickener. Simmer for additional 2 minutes. Transfer cream corn to casserole dish. Sprinkle evenly with cheese. Dot with melted butter and brown under broiler.

EGGPLANT PARMESAN

1-2 small eggplants
1 small jar tomato spaghetti sauce
2 eggs
2 cups cornmeal
1 package grated mozzarella cheese
1 package fresh grated parmesan cheese

Peel and slice eggplant. Soak eggplant after cutting, in salt water for at least 30 minutes to remove bitterness. Beat eggs. Dip eggplant into egg and roll in cornmeal, completely coating pieces. Fry in an iron skillet until brown. Place fried eggplant in baking dish, cover with spaghetti sauce and cheese. Bake in 350 degree oven until cheese is melted and bubbly.

BAKED BEANS

1 large can pork and beans
1 large onion, chopped
1 bell pepper, chopped
5-6 strips of bacon
1 cup brown sugar
1/2 cup catsup
1/2 cup prepared mustard
1/2 cup chow chow

Fry bacon in large skillet. Remove bacon and set aside to use later. Add onion and bell peppers to bacon drippings and cook until onions are transparent. Add beans to onion mixture. Add fried bacon to beans, mix well and pour in baking dish. Top with strips of bacon and bake at 350° for 30 minutes.

Breads

BANANA NUT BREAD

1 box cake mix with butter
3 eggs
1 stick butter, melted
4 mashed bananas
1/2 cup nuts

Mix well and bake in a loaf pan at 350° for 45 minutes to an hour or until golden brown.

OATMEAL 'N' RAISIN MUFFINS

1 cup and 2 tablespoon flour
2 teaspoon double acting baking powder
1/4 teaspoon cinnamon
1/4 teaspoon salt
1/4 cup margarine
1/4 cup firmly packed brown sugar
1/4 cup granulated sugar
1 egg
1 cup skim milk
4 1/2 oz. uncooked quick oats
3/4 cup dark raisins

Combine flour, baking powder, cinnamon and salt, set aside. Cream margarine with sugars until light and fluffy. Add egg and beat until combined. Alternately beat in flour mixture and milk beating well after each addition. Stir in raisins and oats. Fill baking cups in muffin pan with equal amounts of batter about 2/3 full. Bake for 20-25 minutes in a 375° oven.

ZUCCHINI BREAD

3 cups self rising flour
1 teaspoon cinnamon
1 cup salad oil
2 1/2 cups sugar
3 eggs, beaten
2 zucchini, finely chopped
1 teaspoon vanilla
1 cup chopped nuts

Combine flour, cinnamon, oil, sugar and eggs. Mix well. Stir in zucchini, vanilla and nuts. Spoon batter into a lightly greased and floured 9 x 5 x 3 inch loaf pan. Bake for 1 hour or until done in a 350 degree oven. Let cool.

FRENCH BREAKFAST MUFFINS

1/3 cup shortening
1 1/2 cup sugar *(use 1 cup in cinnamon/sugar mixture)*
1 egg
1/2 cup milk
1 1/2 cups flour
1 1/2 teaspoon baking powder
1/2 teaspoon salt
1/2 teaspoon nutmeg
1 teaspoon cinnamon
1/2 cup melted butter

Heat oven to 350°. Grease 15 medium muffin cups. Mix thoroughly shortening, sugar and egg. Stir in flour, baking powder, salt and nutmeg alternately with milk. Fill muffin cups 2/3 full. Bake 20-25 minutes at 350°. Mix 1/2 cup sugar and 1 teaspoon of cinnamon. Immediately after baking, roll muffins in 1/2 cup melted butter, then in the cinnamon-sugar mixture. Serve hot.

ANGEL ROLLS
1 package dry yeast
1/4 cup warm water
2 1/2 to 3 cups flour
1 teaspoon baking powder
1/2 teaspoon soda
1 teaspoon salt
1/2 cup vegetable oil
1 cup buttermilk

Dissolve yeast in warm water. Combine dry ingredients in large bowl. Make a well in the center. Combine milk, oil and yeast mixture and add to dry ingredients. Stir until moistened, will be sticky. Bake rolls at 350° for 16 minutes or until brown.

MAMAW McKINNEY'S HOT ROLLS
1 cup Crisco shortening
1 cup boiling water
3/4 cup sugar
2 well beaten eggs
2 cakes yeast
6 cups self-rising flour

Cream sugar and shortening. Add boiling water, let cool. Dissolve yeast in 1 cup cold water. Add egg and mix, then add yeast mixture, mix well. Add sifted flour. Beat smooth, place in crock and let rise double. Set in refrigerator until ready to use. Take out 2 hours before using. Roll out. Cut with cutter or make in marble size balls. Bake at 350° until golden brown.

CRANBERRY ORANGE BREAD

2 cups sifted flour
grated rind of 1 orange
1 1/2 teaspoon baking powder
3/4 cup fresh or frozen orange juice
1/2 teaspoon soda
1/2 teaspoon salt
1 egg, beaten
1 cup sugar
1 cup halved raw cranberries
2 tablespoon shortening
1 cup chopped pecans

Sift dry ingredients together. Add shortening, rind, orange juice and egg. Mix thoroughly. Fold in cranberries and pecans. Pour into greased loaf pan. Bake at 350° for 1 hour or until toothpick stuck into center comes out clean.

BLUEBERRY MUFFINS

2 cups self rising flour
1/2 cup salad oil
1 cup sugar
1/2 cup milk
2 eggs, slightly beaten
1 cup blueberries
1 teaspoon vanilla extract

Combine flour and sugar in a large bowl and set aside. Combine eggs, vanilla, oil and milk. Make a well in the center of dry ingre-dients, pour in liquids, and stir until well mixed. Fold in blueberries, stir 1 minute. Spoon batter into muffin tins, filling about half full. Bake at 375° for 25 minutes. Makes 2 dozen.

SQUASH SPOON BREAD

1 package Jiffy cornbread mix
2 tablespoon melted margarine
3 cups diced squash
salt and pepper to taste
1 small onion, chopped
cheese, optional
1 cup sour cream

Mix cornbread mix according to directions on box. Add sour cream, squash, onion, salt and pepper. Pour mixture into shallow, ungreased baking dish. Drizzle melted margarine over top. Bake at 350° for 1 hour or until top is browned. Optional: grated cheese may be added.

BUTTERMILK BISCUITS

2 cups self rising flour
1 1/2 teaspoon baking powder
1/4 teaspoon baking soda
1 teaspoon sugar
1/2 cup shortening
1 cup buttermilk

Preheat the oven to 450°. In a large bowl, combine the flour baking powder, soda and sugar. Cut in the shortening with a pastry blender or two knives. Add the buttermilk and knead until smooth and pliable. Roll the dough out on a floured surface to the desired thickness or about 1/2 inch. Cut with a biscuit cutter and place in greased baking pan. Bake for about 12 minutes or until brown on top. Serve with chocolate gravy. (See recipe for gravy on page 140)

PUMPKIN BREAD

3 1/2 cups flour
2 teaspoon baking soda
1 1/2 teaspoon salt
1 teaspoon cinnamon
1 teaspoon nutmeg
2 cups pumpkin
3 cups sugar
1 cup oil
4 eggs
2/3 cup water
1/2 cup nuts-black walnuts are good

Sift dry ingredients in large bowl. Mix well. Add remaining ingredients. Grease 4 coffee cans well and fill each can 1/2 full and place on cookie sheet. Bake at 350° for 1 hour.

FAYE'S PANCAKES

1/2 cup sugar
2 cups self rising flour
1 tablespoon baking powder
1 egg
1 stick butter
milk

Melt butter, add egg, flour sugar, baking powder and enough milk to make batter smooth enough to pour into the skillet. Keep warm in the oven while you fry all the batter.

CORNBREAD

2 cups self rising cornmeal
1 1/2 cups buttermilk
1/3 cup of oil
2 eggs
1 well greased iron skillet, sprinkled with cornmeal

In mixing bowl, mix cornmeal, eggs, buttermilk and oil stirring well. Pour into skillet and place quickly in a pre-heated 500-degree oven and bake 20 minutes or until well browned. Let set for 2-3 minutes, then turn out on plate. Slice and serve.

BLUEBERRY PANCAKES

2 cups flour
2 tablespoon sugar
4 teaspoon baking powder
1 teaspoon salt
2 eggs, slightly beaten
1 1/2 cups milk
1/4 cup salad oil
3/4 cups blueberries, fresh

Combine dry ingredients. Add eggs, milk and salad oil, beat until smooth. Pour batter onto greased griddle. Spoon tablespoon blueberries over each pancake just after pouring batter on griddle.

ONE HOUR ROLLS
3 cups flour
2 tablespoon sugar
1/4 teaspoon soda
1 teaspoon baking powder
1/2 teaspoon salt
3 tablespoon shortening
1 cup buttermilk
1 cake of yeast

Dissolve yeast in buttermilk. Sift salt, sugar, soda and baking powder with flour. Cut shortening in with fork or blender. Add milk and yeast. Work all together lightly. Add more flour if necessary, but keep dough soft. Roll about 1/2 inch thick, cut as you would a biscuit and fold over. Place in pan and let rise 1 hour. Bake for 16-18 minutes in a 350° oven until lightly golden.

VESTAL'S FAMOUS SPOON BISCUITS
(or as Mark Lowry calls them, Cathead Biscuits)
1 cup buttermilk
1/3 cup oil
1 3/4 cup self rising flour
1 large iron skillet

Preheat oven to 400°. Mix all ingredients in mixing bowl until well blended. Spoon biscuit size into well greased skillet. Place in hot oven quickly, do not allow to rise. Cook for 15-20 minutes in hot oven or until as brown as you like them.
(See page 54 for Country Gravy recipe)

VESTAL'S COUNTRY GRAVY

1/2 lb roll sausage
1/3 cup oil
3 heaping tablespoon self rising flour
3 cups milk
1/2 teaspoon black pepper
1/2 teaspoon salt

Fry sausage in oil, pinch into small pieces. Remove sausage and add flour and salt and pepper. Stir well and cook until medium brown. Add milk stirring continually. If needed, add more milk until the consistency you like. Add sausage and serve. Wonderful with spoon biscuits.

Casseroles

HOLIDAY DRESSING

1 large hen
1/2 cup diced celery
1 cup diced onion
2 large skillets of corn bread, cooked
1 can crushed oysters, optional
3 tablespoon black pepper
5 tablespoon sage
6 hard boiled eggs
3 raw eggs, whipped
1 tablespoon salt or to taste
2 sticks of butter

Boil the chicken until tender in a large pot, with full pot of water and two sticks of butter. Remove the meat and allow to cool. Reserve chicken broth. Place corn bread into a large roasting pan for mixing. Break bread into small pieces. Now start adding celery, onions, chopped boiled eggs, whipped eggs, oysters, pepper, sage and salt. Mix well. Add broth 1 cup at a time and continue mixing. Remove chicken from bone and shred. Add at least 2 cups of chicken. Save remaining chicken for your dumplings or giblet gravy. Mix and add broth until mixture is slushy. Pour into well buttered baking pans, this should fill at least 2. If you have too much, grease another pan, ha! Place into a 500°oven and bake approximately 30-45 minutes or until browned to your liking. We like it really brown.

BAKED GRITS
6 cups water
2 1/2 teaspoon salt
1 1/2 cups uncooked grits
3 eggs
1/2 cup butter
4 cups medium cheddar cheese shredded and divided, save 1/4 cup to put on top

Cook grits with water and salt. Melt cheese in grits completely. Beat eggs. Add small amount of hot grits mixture to eggs to temper eggs and then add rest of grits. Put in a 2 1/2 quart casserole dish and top with the 1/4 cup grated cheese. Bake at 350° for 1 hour and 15 minutes, uncovered.

CHICKEN CASSEROLE
1 broiler chicken or four chicken breasts
1 large package egg noodles
1 can cream of chicken soup
1 can cream of mushroom soup
1/2 soup can of water
2 cups buttered bread crumbs

Cook chicken until tender and remove from bone. Cook noodles and drain. Combine noodles, chicken (cut into small pieces), soup, water, salt and pepper to taste. Place in baking dish. Top with buttered breadcrumbs and bake at 350° for 30-45 minutes until brown.

HOT TAMALE CASSEROLE
1 cup plain cornmeal
1 teaspoon salt
1 tablespoon chili powder
2 cups boiling water
1 cup cold water
1 tablespoon shortening

TOPPING:
1 lb ground beef
1/2 cup chopped onion
2 tablespoon flour
1/2 cup ripe olives, chopped
1 lb can tomatoes
1 tablespoon chili powder
3/4 teaspoon salt
1 teaspoon sugar
1/2 cup sharp cheddar cheese, grated

For mush, combine meal, salt, chili powder, shortening and 1 cup cold water. Then add 2 cups boiling water. Cook until thickened. Stir. Cook over low heat 5 minutes covered. Stir. For topping, brown beef, add onion and cook until tender. Add flour, olives, tomatoes, chili powder, salt and sugar. Mix well. Spread mush in 3 quart baking pan and pour topping over it. Add grated cheese on top and bake at 350° for 20 minutes.

CREAMY CHICKEN ENCHILADAS
2 cups chopped cooked chicken
1 cup chopped green pepper
1 jar picante sauce, set 1/2 aside
1 package cream cheese, cubed
(continued on next page)

8 flour tortillas
3/4 lb Velveeta cheese
1/4 cup milk

Stir chicken, green pepper, 1/2 jar of picante sauce and cream cheese in a saucepan over low heat until smooth. Spoon 1/3 cup chicken mixture into each tortilla and roll up. Place seam side down in lightly greased 12 x 8 inch baking pan. Stir cheese spread and milk in saucepan over low heat until smooth. Pour sauce over tortillas and cover with foil. Bake at 350° for 20 minutes or until thoroughly heated. Pour remaining picante sauce over tortillas.

CHICKEN SPAGHETTI

6 boneless chicken breasts, cooked
2 packages spaghetti cooked in chicken broth
1 lb grated American cheese
1 large onion
1 clove garlic, chopped fine
1 cup celery, finely diced
1 green pepper, chopped
2 cans cream of mushroom
1 can pimento, chopped
salt and pepper

Sauté onion, garlic, celery and green peppers in margarine until done. Remove from heat and add soups and pimento. Combine soup mixture, spaghetti and chicken. Mix well. Place half in a lightly greased 4 quart baking dish and top with 1/2 of grated cheese. Put another layer of spaghetti and top with remainder of cheese. Bake at 325° until cheese melts and all is bubbling hot. I usually put 1/2 cup of broth and sometimes a little milk so it doesn't get dry. Serves 12

MACARONI AND CHEESE

1 8 oz. package elbow macaroni
3 tablespoon butter
3 tablespoon flour
2 cups milk
1/2 teaspoon salt
2 cups grated cheddar or American cheese

Cook macaroni according to package directions, drain water and place in a buttered 1 1/2 quarts casserole. Melt butter, stir in flour and blend well. Gradually add milk and cook over a medium heat until thick. Add salt and cheese, stirring to melt cheese. Gently mix sauce with macaroni. Bake uncovered at 350° for 30 minutes.

CHICKEN POT PIE

6 chicken breasts or 2 fryers
1/2 cup chopped celery
1 chopped onion
5 carrots, sliced
6 medium potatoes
1 can small early peas
1/3 cup flour
3/4 cup butter
1/2 cup milk
salt and pepper
canned biscuits

Boil chicken. When done, remove chicken from pot and strain broth. Put strained broth back into pot. Skin and debone chicken and cut in chunks. Add chicken, celery, onion and carrots to (continued on next page) broth. Add potatoes and cook until potatoes are tender. Add peas, salt and pepper. Add 1/2 cup butter to broth and vegetables. Use remainder of butter to butter baking dish. Mix flour and milk to make paste. Add flour paste to broth, stirring as it thickens. Put in casserole dish and top with biscuits and bake in 350° oven until biscuits are brown.

MEMAW'S MEATLOAF

2 lb ground beef
1 large onion
2 eggs
chopped celery
tomato juice
catsup
cracker crumbs
salt and pepper

Mix all ingredients. Form into loaf. Lay bell pepper rings on top to bake, then remove. Bake at 400° approximately 1/2 hour and then at 350° for 1/2 hour.

CHICKEN CASSEROLE

1 package Pepperidge farm cornbread stuffing mix
1 stick margarine
1 can cream of mushroom soup
1 can cream of chicken soup
4 large chicken breasts

Boil chicken, save broth. Debone chicken. Melt margarine and stir into dressing. In greased dish, put layer of dressing, layer of chicken, layer of soup diluted with 1 can of broth. Keep layering ending with stuffing mix. Bake at 350° for 45 minutes to an hour or until brown.

CHILI RELLENO CASSEROLE
1 lb ground beef
1/2 cup chopped onions
1/2 teaspoon salt
1/4 teaspoon pepper
2 cans green chilies
1 1/2 cups shredded cheddar cheese
1/4 cup all purpose flour
4-6 eggs beaten
1 1/2 cups milk

Brown beef and onions, drain well. Sprinkle meat with salt and pepper. Put one half of chilies in the bottom of a greased baking dish. Sprinkle with cheese and top with meat. Arrange rest of chilies over top of meat. Set aside. Mix flour and salt in bowl, combine with eggs and milk, adding gradually and beating until smooth. Pour over top of chili and meat mixture. Bake at 350° or until knife inserted in center comes out clean. Let stand for 5-10 minutes, cut into squares and serve.

OVEN STEW
2 lb stew meat
1 large or 2 medium onions
3 stalks celery cut in chunks
2 medium carrots
2 beef bouillon
1/3 cup minute tapioca
1 tablespoon sugar
1 teaspoon salt
1/4 teaspoon pepper
(continued on next page)

2 cups tomato juice
1 bay leaf
3 large potatoes

Combine all ingredients except potatoes, cover and bake 5 hours at 250°. Add potatoes last hour.

BREAKFAST SAUSAGE CASSEROLE

1 lb sausage cooked, crumbled and drained
10 eggs beaten
3 cups light cream
1/2 teaspoon salt
1/2 cup chopped green onions
1 teaspoon dry mustard
1 1/2 cups cubed bread crumbs
1 cup shredded cheddar cheese
1 cup shredded Swiss cheese

Place bread in well greased 9 x 13 inch pan. Mix all ingredients, pour over cubed bread crumbs and sprinkle with cheese. Refrigerate overnight. Bake at 350° for 1 hour or until golden brown.

LASAGNA

1 can tomato paste
1 large can tomato sauce
2 tablespoon sugar
(1) 16 oz. carton creamed cottage cheese
1 egg
1 tablespoon parsnips
1 teaspoon salt
1 pound mozzarella cheese
1 teaspoon oregano
2 lb ground beef
1 box lasagna noodles

Cook ground beef. Mix tomato paste, sauce and sugar. Cook the noodles, run cold water over them when they are done. Put a little sauce mixture in the bottom of the pan and add a little meat. Layer the noodles on top of meat. Mix cottage cheese, egg, parsnips, salt and oregano together. Spread half of the mixture over the noodles, add half of the mozzarella cheese, layer of meat, layer of sauce, layer of noodles, the other half of the cottage cheese mixture and the last of the mozzarella cheese. Cover with foil and bake at 375° for 25 minutes. Remove foil and bake for 25 minutes. Let cool for 15-30 minutes.

CAVATINI

3 of the following uncooked pastas; 1 cup rigatoni, 1 cup mostoccioli, 1/2 cup rotini, 1/2 cup shell macaroni
1 lb ground beef
1 medium onion, chopped
1 medium green pepper, chopped
3 oz. pepperoni, sliced
(1) 15 1/2 oz. jar spaghetti sauce
1 cup cream style cottage cheese
8 oz. mozzarella cheese, grated

Preheat oven to 350°. Cook pasta according to package directions. Drain well. While pasta is cooking, brown ground beef with onion and green pepper until onion is transparent. Stir in pepperoni and cook until just heated. Drain fat. Add spaghetti sauce. Simmer 5 minutes. Arrange half the pasta in a lightly greased 3 quart baking dish. Spoon on half of meat sauce. Spread cottage cheese over the sauce. Sprinkle with half of the mozzarella cheese. Repeat layers, omitting cottage cheese. Bake uncovered 30-35 minutes.

CHICKEN VEGETABLE CASSEROLE

4-6 chicken breast
flour for coating
1/2 cup shortening
1/2 teaspoon salt
1/2 teaspoon black pepper
1/2 teaspoon red pepper
4 large potatoes, peeled and quartered
1 large bell pepper, cut in strips
1 large onion, chopped
1 can mushrooms
1 can cream of mushroom soup

Dredge chicken in flour and brown in shortening. Remove from skillet to baking dish with cover. Add potatoes, pepper and onion. Sprinkle with salt and pepper over top. Mix mushrooms with mushroom soup and pour over chicken and vegetables. Bake 45 minutes at 350° or until vegetables are tender. Serve with salad and rolls.

CHICKEN DIVAN

3 or 4 cups cooked rice (white or brown)
3 whole chicken breasts, boiled until done and cubed
1 can cream of chicken soup
3/4 lb Velveeta cheese, cubed
1 lb frozen or fresh broccoli

Butter 9 x 13 pan. Spread rice in bottom of dish. Spread chicken over rice. Place broccoli on top of chicken. Mix soup and cheese. Pour cheese and soup mixture over broccoli. Bake for 30 minutes at 350°.

CHICKEN ENCHILADAS

cooking oil
12 (6) inch corn tortillas
2 cups chopped cooked chicken
2 4 oz. cans diced green chili peppers
1/2 cup chopped red or green onion
1 cup salsa
1 8 oz. carton dairy sour cream
2 cups shredded Monterey Jack cheese

Heat 2 tablespoons of cooking oil in a medium skillet. Holding a tortilla with tongs, dip each in hot oil 5-10 seconds, or until limp. Drain on a paper towel. Repeat with remaining tortillas, adding more oil if necessary. Combine chicken, chilies, onion and salsa. Spoon about 1/4 cup chicken mixture on each tortilla. Roll up. Place tortilla rolls seam side down, in a baking dish. Bake covered in a 350° oven for 20-25 minutes. Uncover and spread sour cream atop. Sprinkle with cheese and bake 5 minutes longer or until cheese melts.

PARTY EGGS

3 dozen eggs
1 1/3 cups light cream
3 teaspoon salt
1/4 cup butter
2 cups medium white sauce (see recipe on page 67)
chopped parsley
add pepper to taste

Beat eggs with cream, salt and pepper. Melt butter in large frying pan. Pour in egg mixture, stirring occasionally until almost set. Fold in hot white sauce, while eggs are still creamy. Keep hot in a very slow oven or place over hot water on top of range. Sprinkle with parsley. These eggs are great for late night breakfast.

MEDIUM WHITE CREAM SAUCE
1/4 cup butter
1/4 cup flour
1 teaspoon salt
1/8 teaspoon pepper
2 cups milk or half & half

In heavy saucepan, heat butter until melted. Remove from heat and add flour, salt and pepper, stirring constantly until smooth texture. Add milk slowly, stirring constantly, and return to medium heat. Bring to a boil and cook one minute, stirring constantly.

CHICKEN BREASTS IN SOUR CREAM GRAVY
10 deboned chicken breasts
salt and pepper
paprika
1/2 cup butter
1 can cream of mushroom soup
1 carton sour cream
1 can fried onion rings

Salt and pepper chicken and sprinkle with lots of paprika. Top with butter patties and bake at 350° for 1 hour. Reserve chicken and make gravy in drippings with the mushroom soup and sour cream. Return chicken to baking dish and pour mushroom gravy over the top. Put onion rings on top of gravy and bake 20 minutes more.

BACON WRAPPED CHICKEN BREAST
1 jar dried beef
1 cup sour cream
1 can mushroom soup
6 chicken breasts, boneless and skinless
6 strips bacon

Line baking dish with dried beef. Wrap bacon around chicken. Mix soup and sour cream. Pour over chicken and let set, covered in refrigerator overnight. Bake at 275-300° for 3 hours. Uncover and cook 20-30 minutes more to brown. Serve over hot rice with salad.

SWEET AND SOUR CHICKEN
6-8 chicken breasts, skinless/boneless

In flat pan, put chicken, meat side up.

In bowl, mix:
1 bottle Russian dressing
1 jar apricot preserves or orange marmalade
1 package onion soup mix

Spread mixture over chicken, cover, and bake 1 1/4 hours at 350°.

AUNTIE'S THICK SLAB BACON

Roll bacon in flour, covering well. Shake off excess. Fry in iron skillet in small amount of oil until golden brown. Drain on paper towels. Serve with drop biscuits and thickening milk gravy.

GIBLET GRAVY

8 cups good chicken broth, preferably from your dressing and dumpling hen or turkey
1 cup raw dressing
1 cup chicken or turkey giblets or meat well chopped
2 tablespoon black pepper
salt to taste
3 hard boiled eggs
3 raw whipped eggs

Place broth in large saucepan. Bring to a boil. Reduce heat and add chopped boiled eggs, whipped eggs, pepper, chopped chicken and uncooked dressing. Stir frequently. Mix together in a separate bowl, 1 cup milk, 2 tablespoons corn starch and slowly add until gravy is the consistency you like. It will be even better if you add 1 cup evaporated milk. Enjoy darlin's! We do!

Main Dishes

CHICKEN DIJON

4 or 6 chicken breasts
8 oz. sour cream
4 tablespoon spicy brown mustard
seasoned breadcrumbs

Mix sour cream and mustard. Roll chicken in mixture, cover well, then roll in seasoned breadcrumbs. Line oblong pan with foil, enough to cover chicken. Place chicken in the lined pan, place a pat of butter or oleo on each piece of chicken, cover and seal foil over chicken. Cook for 30 minutes at 350°, then uncover and cook 15 minutes at 450°.

BARBECUED HAMBURGERS

1 lb ground beef
1/2 cup uncooked rolled oats
2/3 cup pet milk
3 teaspoon cut onion
1 teaspoon salt
1 teaspoon pepper
1/2 cup catsup
1/2 cup barbecue sauce

Mix all ingredients in large bowl. With your hands, shape mixture into patties. Brown slowly. Spread meat with catsup and bottled barbecue sauce. Cover and cook 5 minutes longer.

CHICKEN & DUMPLINGS

16 cups broth (at least)
1 hen, boiled and chopped
(continued on next page)

2 eggs, whipped
2 cans evaporated milk
2 sticks butter
1 1/2 cups broth
2 1/2 cups all purpose flour

Place 16 cups broth and evaporated milk in large pan. Add butter, whipped eggs and chopped chicken. Now in mixing bowl, mix the 1 1/2 cups broth and all purpose flour, stir well. This should be stiff, if not add more flour. Separate into three equal portions. On well floured wax paper, use self-rising flour for this, place one wad on paper and sprinkle with flour. Roll dough out with rolling pin and cut into 1 inch slices. Pinch or cut into two pieces and drop a few at a time into boiling broth. Continue this process until you have used all your dough. Be sure to dunk the dumplings frequently, and stir gently from the bottom. Let simmer on low heat for 10 to 20 minutes. Add 2 tablespoons of black pepper and salt to taste.

SLOPPY JOE'S
2 lb hamburger
2/3 cup chili sauce
1 tablespoon yellow mustard
1 tablespoon chili powder
1 diced onion
salt and pepper to taste

Mix all ingredients and cook in a double boiler for 1 hour stirring occasionally. Makes 16 sloppy Joe's.

OVEN FRIED CHICKEN

1/4 cup butter
1 clove garlic, minced
2 teaspoon salt
1/8 teaspoon pepper
2 cups dry bread crumbs
3/4 cup Parmesan cheese
1/4 cup minced parsley
1 fryer, cut up or 6 chicken breasts, skinned

Melt butter with garlic in it. Combine salt, pepper, crumbs, cheese and parsley. Dip chicken pieces in butter, then in crumbs. Lay in shallow baking pan. Do not overlap. Do not turn. Bake uncovered at 350° for 1 hour.

CRUSTLESS QUICHE

8 eggs, slightly beaten
6 slices bread, cubed
2 cups milk
1 lb sausage, cooked and crumbled
1 cup cheddar cheese, grated
1 teaspoon salt
1 teaspoon dry mustard

Mix together and refrigerate 6 hours or overnight. Bake at 350° for 45 minutes in an oiled 7 x 11 pan.

MEXICAN QUICHE

5 cups cheddar cheese, grated
4 cups Monterey Jack, grated
2 medium tomatoes
1 can diced green chilies
1 can black olives, drained
2 tablespoon flour
2 unbaked pie shells
6 eggs
1/2 cup flour
2 cups half & half
1/2 teaspoon salt
1/4 teaspoon cumin
1/2 teaspoon oregano leaves
1/2 teaspoon pepper

Mix cheese, tomatoes, chilies and olives with flour. Mix well. Spoon into piecrust. Beat eggs. Blend 1/2 cup flour and half-and-half with eggs. Beat until smooth. Add salt, cumin, oregano and pepper. Mix well and pour over cheese mixture. Bake until golden and firm in a 350-degree oven.

FANCY EGG SCRAMBLE
1 cup diced Canadian bacon
1/4 cup chopped green onion
3 tablespoon butter, melted
1 recipe cheese sauce (see recipe below)
2 1/4 cup soft bread crumbs
12 beaten eggs
1 can mushrooms, drained
1/8 teaspoon paprika

In large skillet, cook bacon and onions in butter until onions are tender. Add eggs and scramble until just set. Fold mushrooms and eggs into cheese sauce. Pour into baking dish. Combine melted butter, breadcrumbs and paprika to sprinkle over eggs. Cover and chill until 30 minutes before serving. Bake uncovered for 30 minutes in a 350° oven.

CHEESE SAUCE
2 tablespoon butter
2 tablespoon flour
1/2 teaspoon salt
1/8 teaspoon pepper
2 cups milk
1 cup grated cheese

Melt butter. Blend in flour, salt and pepper. Add milk. Cook and stir until bubbly. Stir in cheese.

CRUST FOR QUICHE

1 1/2 cups flour
dash salt
1/2 cup oil
2 1/2 teaspoon milk

Mix and press into pan.

HAMBURGER STROGANOFF

1 1/2 lbs ground beef
1 large onion, chopped
1 jar mushrooms
1 can beef broth
1 tablespoon Worcestershire sauce
1 teaspoon garlic powder
1 can cream of mushroom soup
1 carton of sour cream

Brown meat in skillet with salt and pepper. Add onion and cook until tender. Add mushrooms and beef broth. Add Worcestershire sauce, garlic powder and cream of mushroom soup. Stir and cook about 20 minutes. Add a small carton of sour cream and cook for about 5 minutes. Serve over hot buttered noodles or rice. Garnish with dried parsley flakes sprinkled over top.

SALMON PATTIES
1 large can salmon, undrained
1 grated carrot
2 eggs, beaten
1/2 cup flour

Mix all ingredients. Spoon a heaping tablespoon of salmon mixture into a medium hot iron skillet of oil. Fry patties turning often until golden brown.

FAYE'S PORK CHOPS
2 cans fruit cocktail
6 pork chops

Sear pork chops. Pour fruit cocktail over pork chops. Cook at 200° in electric skillet for approximately 30 minutes or until tender.

CRANBERRY CHICKEN
8-9 chicken breast
1 bottle Russian dressing
1 envelope onion soup
1 can whole berry cranberry sauce

Mix dressing, onion soup and cranberry sauce. Pour over chicken breasts and bake uncovered for 1 hour at 350°.

SEAFOOD FOR 10
1 lb crab
2 lb shrimp
1/2 cup butter
1/2 cup flour
4 cups milk
2 teaspoon salt
mushrooms, fresh or canned
1 tablespoon celery flakes
1/2 cup chopped green peppers
1/3 cup chopped onion
1/2 cup chopped black olives
1 1/2 teaspoon pimento
4 cups grated mild cheese

Sauté mushrooms, celery flakes, chopped green pepper, onion, black olives, pimento. Melt butter, stir in flour and milk to make white sauce. Add sautéed vegetables to white sauce. Add cheese and crab until cheese melts. Add cooked shrimp last and leave on very low heat or remove from heat. To cook shrimp, I put them in boiling water and remove almost instantly as they turn pink. Serve over rice.

CLASSIC SPAGHETTI AND MEATBALLS

MEATBALLS:
1 1/2 lbs ground beef
1/2 cup fine dry bread crumbs
1/4 cup freshly grated Parmesan cheese
1 1/2 teaspoon salt
1/2 teaspoon basil
1/4 teaspoon pepper
1 egg, slightly beaten
1/4 cup warm water
olive oil

SAUCE:
1 28 oz. can whole tomatoes with juice, chopped
1/4 cup chopped onion
2 tablespoon chopped fresh parsley
2 cloves garlic, minced
1 teaspoon salt
1 teaspoon oregano
1/4 teaspoon anise seed
1 6oz. can tomato paste
12 oz. spaghetti, cooked according to package and drained
freshly grated parmesan cheese

Combine all ingredients for meatballs and roll into thirty six 1 inch balls. In large skillet, brown meatballs slowly in a small amount of olive oil. Add tomatoes, onion, parsley, garlic, salt, oregano, anise and tomato paste to meatballs and simmer uncovered 1 1/2 - 2 hours or until thick. Stir occasionally. Serve over spaghetti and sprinkle with Parmesan cheese.

VEGETABLE BEEF STEW

4 lbs stew beef
10 potatoes
10 carrots or 2 cups chopped
1 cup chopped celery
1 cup chopped onions
1 teaspoon Lawry's seasoning salt
1 teaspoon black pepper
1 tablespoon sugar
1/3 teaspoon cumin

In large pan, cook meat in 2 quarts of water on medium heat for 2 hours. Add vegetables and seasonings. Cook another hour, add water if needed, then simmer 10 minutes. You may add a can of tomatoes or catsup if you want a tomato taste. Delicious served with cornbread.

NEW ORLEANS STYLE BARBECUE SHRIMP

10 lbs headless in shell shrimp
3 lbs butter
1/2 cup cooking oil
1 lemon, sliced thin
2 tablespoon minced garlic
1/2 teaspoon salt
3 heaping tablespoon black pepper
1/2 teaspoon file gumbo spice
5 tablespoon spicy cajun mix
3 tablespoon roux and gravy

In heavy pot or pan, melt butter and oil, add sliced lemon and all spices, stirring very often. Simmer for 20-30 minutes. Have shrimp washed and drained. Add shrimp. Cook on medium heat for 20-30 minutes or until shrimp are done. I serve mine in soup bowls with plenty of the roux, or gravy, with extra bowls for the shells and plenty of French bread for sopping the gravy. No need for anything else on the table. No one's gonna eat anything but shrimp, bread and gravy. 'Course your gonna need lots of napkins and bibs for this one!

SWEET AND SOUR PORK

6-8 pork chops
1 can chunk pineapple
1/2 lemon thinly sliced
4 tablespoon soy sauce
3 tablespoon oil
1 can sliced water chestnuts
1 can sliced mushrooms
(continued on next page)

1/2 cup flour
1/2 cup black pepper
3 tablespoon sugar

Place oil in skillet. Flour and pepper on wax paper, mix well and roll pork on both sides in flour. Fry in medium heat skillet with oil until brown on both sides. Place in large pot on medium heat and add pineapple, juice and all, lemon, soy sauce, water chestnuts, mushrooms and sugar. Stir well and simmer for 30 minutes. Serve over steamed rice. Very delicious!

SWEET AND SOUR RICE

2 sticks of butter
1 cup diced carrots
1/2 cup diced celery
1/2 cup chopped onions
1 can chunk pineapple, drained
1 can sliced water chestnuts, drained
2 cups minute rice, prepared according to
   instructions on package
4 tablespoon soy sauce
2 tablespoon sugar

In large Dutch oven type pot, heat butter and carrots, celery and onions. Sauté for 3-5 minutes, add water chestnuts, soy sauce, sugar and pineapple. Add to cooked rice, stir and mix well. It is now ready to eat. This goes great with any meal. Leftovers may be stored in refrigerator, this will keep for a week, so reheat in the microwave and enjoy!

STEAK AND RICE
2 medium onions, chopped
2 lbs round steak
3 teaspoon Worchester sauce
2 medium bell peppers, chopped
1 can beefy onion soup
1 can water
2 tablespoon flour

Sauté onions and bell pepper in microwave with a pat of butter while browning steak. Slice steak into small pieces. Return meat, onions and bell peppers to skillet. Add onion soup, water and 2 tablespoons of flour. Cook over low heat for approximately 20 minutes until thick. erve over rice or noodles.

CREOLE SHRIMP
3 lbs cleaned, de-veined shrimp
1 stick margarine
8 oz. can mushrooms
garlic powder to taste
red pepper to taste
4 cups cooked rice

Place cleaned shrimp in single layer on broiler pan dotted with margarine. Turn shrimp over when they turn pink. Add mushrooms to shrimp and sprinkle with garlic and red pepper. Broil on other side until pink. Serve over rice with salad and garlic bread.

OVEN BARBECUED CHICKEN

1 cup up chicken or chicken breasts
flour for coating chicken
3/4 cup margarine or butter
1/2 cup white vinegar
1 teaspoon salt
1/2 teaspoon black pepper
1/2 teaspoon red pepper
2 tablespoon Worcestershire sauce
1 teaspoon dry mustard
1/2 teaspoon paprika
1/2 teaspoon garlic powder

Melt margarine in large non-stick skillet over medium heat. Dredge chicken in flour and brown on all sides in melted margarine. Watch carefully so it doesn't burn. Remove chicken from pan to a baking dish. Add the other ingredients to the drippings in skillet, stir to loosen browned particles and pour over chicken. Bake covered with foil for 45 minutes at 350°. Uncover and bake 15 more minutes.

FETTUCCINI ALFREDO

1 lb fettuccini noodles, cooked
1/2 cup Parmesan cheese
1 pint of whipping cream
1/4 cup blue cheese
1/2 stick butter
dash white pepper

Melt butter, then melt blue cheese. Add whipping cream and white pepper. Let boil and then add Parmesan cheese. Pour over noodles.

Family & Friends

Jake and I in Hawaii, playing with Jake's Grandbaby, JakeIII

Family at the Thanksgiving table - 1987

Howard at a Sunday dinner on The Ground Meeting - 1978.

Setting the table for a friend - 1970.

Vestal and Sydney at Sydney's first birthday party.

A wonderful family outing.

My dear friend Betty and I sharing our birthday with the family.

After the concert, Howard is on the bus and ready for bed, but not before a midnight snack with David Phelps.

Enjoying a quite moment.

A picture is worth a thousand words. Here's George and I on a bicycle built for two.

The cast of The Gospel Singing Jubilee having dinner - 1967.

Momma, Daddy & family - 1967.

The Happy Goodman Family Reunion Dinner - 1968.

Here I am in deep thought.

Mamma & Howard in Hawaii - 1970.

Howard's favorite past-time - 1976.

Mark and I on the bus recouping after a concert.

Christmas with Family - 1991.

I caught a trout!
Colorado - 1996.

Desserts

VESTAL'S TOFFEE
1 lb butter or oleo
1 lb brown sugar
3/4 cup chocolate chips or 3 Hershey's bars
3/4 cup finely chopped pecans or pecan meal

Cook butter and sugar in iron skillet to 300° on candy thermometer, stirring constantly. Quickly pour on lightly greased cookie sheet and spread. Sprinkle chips and spread as chocolate melts. Sprinkle nuts and let cool completely, then pop out of pan and break into small pieces.

BREAD PUDDING
3-4 teaspoon soft butter
3/4 cup brown sugar
4 slices soft white bread with no crust
4 eggs
1 cup half & half
1 cup milk
2 teaspoon vanilla
1/4 cup sugar
1/2 teaspoon cinnamon
1/4 teaspoon nutmeg

In a casserole dish, rub with 1 teaspoon butter. Press brown sugar into dish about a 1/8 inch shell. Butter bread and cut into 1 inch cubes and press into brown sugar shell, butter side down. Mix eggs, milk, half-and-half, vanilla and sugar. Pour mixture over bread and cover tightly with foil. In large pot, fill 1/2 full with water and bring to a boil. Put casserole into pan of boiling water so it goes up about 3/4 of the way. Sprinkle with cinnamon and nutmeg and cover tightly with foil. Cook 1 1/2 hours. Keep adding water if necessary. Dump upside down and serve with whipped cream.

CHOCOLATE PECAN PIE

3 eggs, slightly beaten
1 cup light corn syrup
1/2 cup sugar
1/2 cup semisweet chocolate chips
2 tablespoon butter or margarine
1 teaspoon vanilla
1 1/2 cups pecan halves
1 unbaked 9 inch pie shell

In large bowl, stir eggs, corn syrup, sugar, chocolate chips, butter and vanilla until well blended. Stir in pecans. Pour into pie shell. Bake for 50-60 minutes in 350-degree oven until knife inserted halfway between center and edge comes out clean. Cool on wire rack.

CHOCOLATE FUDGE

3 6oz. packages semi-sweet chocolate chips
1 14oz. can sweetened condensed milk
dash of salt
1 1/2 teaspoon vanilla
1/2 cup chopped nuts (optional)

In heavy saucepan, over low heat, melt chips with condensed milk. Remove from heat and stir in remaining ingredients. Spread evenly into wax paper-lined 8 inch square pan. Chill 2 or 3 hours until firm. Turn fudge onto cutting board and peel off paper. Cut into 1 inch squares. Store loosely covered at room temperature.

LEMON CAKE
1 lemon cake mix
4 eggs
1/2 cup oil
1 small box lemon pudding
1 16oz. bottle 7-UP

Mix all ingredients and pour into greased and floured bundt pan. Bake 50-60 minutes at 325°.

GLAZE:
1/2 cup lemon juice
2 tbs melted butter
2 cups powdered sugar

Mix ingredients well. Drizzle over cooled cake.

MOLASSES COOKIES
1/2 cup shortening
3/4 cup sugar
1 egg
1 1/4 cups molasses
4 1/2 cups flour
2 teaspoon soda
1 teaspoon salt
2 teaspoon ginger
1 teaspoon cinnamon
1 teaspoon nutmeg
1 teaspoon cloves
1 cup boiling water

Combine shortening, sugar, egg and molasses. Mix well. (continued on next page)

Sift together flour, soda, salt, ginger, cinnamon, nutmeg and cloves. Mix with combined mixture. Add water stirring until smooth. Drop by teaspoonfuls onto lightly greased cookie sheet. Bake for 8-10 minutes at 400-degrees.

FROSTING:
2 cups confectioner's sugar
1 tablespoon butter
1 teaspoon lemon extract
3 tablespoon milk

Combine all ingredients, beat until smooth and ice cookies.

CHRISTMAS DONUTS
1 cup sugar
1 cup mashed potatoes
1 egg
1/2 cup milk
1 tablespoon melted butter
3 cups and 2 tablespoons flour
2 1/2 teaspoon baking powder

Mix well and drop into hot cooking oil and fry until brown and crispy. Cool on brown paper bag. Roll in mixture of sugar and cinnamon.

BANANA PUDDING

2 cups sugar
1½ cups self-rising flour
1 large can pet milk
2 1/2 cup homogenized milk
1 tablespoon vanilla
3 eggs
1 box vanilla wafers
6 large ripe bananas

Mix well in heavy saucepan, sugar and flour. Add milk and vanilla, beat until well blended and no lumps. Cook over low heat, stirring almost continually until it begins to thicken. Whip eggs and add to sauce, stir until smooth, almost thick gravy consistency. Have bananas sliced ahead of time. In large bowl, layer vanilla wafers and bananas, pour hot sauce over layer and repeat. Let wafers and bananas soak for a few minutes and then have a ball!

PUMPKIN PIE

1 9 inch unbaked pie shell
1 can pumpkin
1 can condensed sweetened milk
2 eggs
1 teaspoon cinnamon
1 teaspoon ginger
1 teaspoon nutmeg
1/2 teaspoon salt

Beat eggs, pumpkin and milk together. Add the other ingredients and pour into pie shell. Bake 45-50 minutes at 350° or until set.

JAM CAKE

5 eggs
2 cups sugar
3 cups flour
1 cup butter
1 cup buttermilk
1 teaspoon soda
1/2 teaspoon salt
1/2 teaspoon cinnamon
1 1/2 teaspoon cloves
1 1/2 teaspoon allspice
1 cup raisins
1 cup chopped nuts
1 cup jam

TOPPING:
1/2 cup sugar
1 teaspoon of cinnamon

Cream butter, add sugar. Beat eggs well and gradually add to butter mixture. Sift spices with flour. Dissolve soda in buttermilk and add to flour mixture. Gradually add flour mixture to butter and sugar mixture, mixing well after each addition. Mix in nuts, raisins and jam. Bake at 350° until fork comes clean.

JAM CAKE ICING:
2 cups sugar
3/4 cup pet milk
1 stick butter

In saucepan, cook for 2 minutes and beat until right consistency to spread.

PECAN PIE

2 tablespoon flour
3 eggs
3 packages chopped pecans
2 cup sugar
1/4 cup corn syrup
1 teaspoon vanilla
9 inch pie shell

Blend flour and sugar. Add eggs, syrup, nuts and vanilla. Pour into shallow 9 inch pie shell. Bake 45 minutes in 350 degree oven.

FRUIT COCKTAIL CAKE
1 cup flour
1 teaspoon soda
1 teaspoon salt
1 cup sugar
1 teaspoon cinnamon
1 egg
1 can fruit cocktail
1/2 cup walnuts or almonds
whip cream, optional

Mix all ingredients except brown sugar and nuts together. Pour in a square 8 inch baking pan. Sprinkle brown sugar and nuts on top and bake at 300° for 1 hour. Top with whipped cream if desired.

DOUBLE CHOCOLATE FANTASY BARS
1 package chocolate cake mix
1/3 cup oil
1 egg
1 cup chopped nuts
1 can sweetened condensed milk
1 package semi-sweet chocolate chips
1 teaspoon vanilla extract
dash of salt

In a large mixing bowl, beat cake mix, oil and egg on medium speed until crumbly. Add nuts. Reserving 1 1/2 cups of crumb mixture, press remainder firmly on bottom of greased 13 x 9 inch pan. In small saucepan, combine remaining ingredients. Over medium heat, cook and stir until chips melt. Pour evenly over prepared crust. Top with reserved crumb mixture. Bake 25-30 minutes in a 350-degree oven or until bubbly. Cool and cut into bars. Store loosely covered at room temperature.

COOKIE FROSTING
4oz. cream cheese
2 tablespoon honey
1 teaspoon vanilla
2 tablespoon butter

Cream all ingredients together well. Makes enough for about one batch of cookies. May be doubled as desired.

DATE BARS
1/4 cup butter or margarine
1/2 cup honey
2 teaspoon vanilla
2 eggs
1 cup whole wheat flour
3/4 teaspoon baking powder
1/4 teaspoon salt
1/2 teaspoon coriander
1 1/2 cups dates
1 cup walnuts

Preheat oven to 350°. Cream together honey and butter, add vanilla and eggs and beat well. In another bowl, combine whole-wheat flour, baking powder, salt and coriander. Add flour mixture to liquid mixture and stir to combine. Stir in dates and nuts. Grease and flour a 9 x 13 inch baking pan, preferably metal. Spread batter on the bottom. The batter will be thick and will take a little work to spread it evenly. Place in a hot oven and bake for 25-30 minutes or until lightly browned. When slightly cooled, cut and remove from the pan. When completely cooled the bars may be frosted with cookie frosting.

STRAWBERRY DELIGHT

1 9oz. angel food cake
1 8oz. package of cream cheese
1 cup whole milk
1 can strawberry pie filling, chilled
1 9oz. carton cool whip

Crumble cake into oblong Pyrex dish. Blend softened cream cheese and milk. Pour cheese mixture over crumbled cake and let stand in refrigerator 1 1/2-2 hours. Spread chilled pie filling onto mixture, then top with cool whip and refrigerate until time to serve. NOTE: You may substitute the strawberry pie filling for blueberry filling. Both are delicious.

COCONUT KISSES

1/2 cup egg whites
1 1/4 cups sugar
1 teaspoon salt
1/2 teaspoon vanilla
2 1/2 cups moist shredded coconut

Beat egg whites until frothy. Gradually beat in sugar. Continue beating until very stiff and glossy. Stir in remaining ingredients. Drop teaspoonfuls of mixture 2 inches apart on ungreased waxed paper on baking sheet. Bake until set and delicately brown in a 325° oven.

TURTLE PIE
(1) 9 inch baked pastry shell
12 unwrapped caramel candies
1 can sweetened condensed milk
2 squares unsweetened chocolate
1/4 cup margarine
2 eggs
2 tablespoon water
1 teaspoon vanilla extract
dash of salt
1/2 cup chopped pecans

In small heavy saucepan, over low heat, melt caramels with 1/3 cup sweetened condensed milk. Spread evenly on bottom of prepared pastry shell. In medium saucepan, over low heat, melt chocolate with margarine. In large bowl, beat eggs with remaining milk, water, vanilla and salt. Add chocolate mixture, mix well. Pour into prepared shell. Top with pecans and bake 35 minutes or until center is done in a 325° oven. Cool. Chill. Refrigerate leftovers.

7 MINUTE FROSTING
3 egg whites
1/2 cup white corn syrup
1 cup sugar
1/2 teaspoon cream of tartar

[Handwritten note: Mix + Cook in double boiler for 7 min (peaks will form). Beat on high continually.]

Cook together in a double boiler on medium heat. Mix on high speed until it forms peaks.

GRAHAM CRACKER CAKE

2 cups sugar
1 cup shortening
5 whole eggs
1 lb graham cracker crumbs
2 teaspoon baking powder
1 cup sweet milk
1 tablespoon vanilla
1 cup coconut
1 cup nuts, chopped fine

Cream sugar and shortening, add eggs. Beat until well blended. Add baking powder, crumbs, milk, coconut, vanilla and nuts. Bake in 3 layer pans for 30-35 minutes at 325°.

ICING:
Blend 1 stick butter, 1 box confectioners sugar and 1 large can crushed pineapple, drained well. Spread on cooled cake.

CREAMY RICE PUDDING

1/2 cup uncooked rice
3 cups boiling water
1 can sweetened condensed milk
1/2 cup raisins
2 eggs
1 teaspoon vanilla
1/2 teaspoon nutmeg, if desired

Put rice in water, use heavy saucepan, cook over medium heat until done. Remove from heat, stir in raisins and milk. Add beaten eggs slowly, stirring well. Return to low heat and cook, stirring constantly until mixture coats on metal spoon. Remove from heat and stir in vanilla. Serve hot or cold.

AUNT BEA'S FRUIT CAKE

3 8oz. packages pitted dates
1 lb candied pineapple
1 lb whole candied cherries
2 cups sifted all purpose flour
2 teaspoon baking powder
1/2 teaspoon salt
4 eggs
1 cup granulated sugar
2 lb pecan halves

Preheat oven to 270°. Grease tube pan with oil or butter, line pan with brown paper or oil paper. Cut dates and pineapple in coarse pieces. In a large bowl, combine dates, pineapple and cherries. In separate bowl, mix flour, salt and baking powder. Mix dry ingredients with fruit and mix with hands, making sure all pieces are covered with flour. In small bowl, beat eggs until frothy, gradually beat in 1 cup sugar. Add eggs to fruit mixture, mix well. Add nuts and mix with hands until nuts are evenly distributed and are coated with batter. Pack into pan, pressing down with palms of hands. Decorate top with cherries and pecans. Bake 1 1/2 hours. Let set 5 minutes. Turn out on plate, carefully peel paper off and turn upside down. Brush with corn syrup. This seams hard, but is actually very simple and is not your average fruit cake!

RICH LEMON BARS
1 1/2 cups plus 3 tablespoon flour
1/2 cup powdered sugar
3/4 cup cold margarine
4 eggs, slightly beaten
1/2 cup granulated sugar
1 teaspoon baking powder
1/2 cup lemon juice
additional powdered sugar

In medium bowl, combine 1 1/2 cups flour and powdered sugar, cut in margarine until crumbly. Press into bottom of lightly greased 13 x 9 inch baking pan, bake 15 minutes in 350 degree oven. Meanwhile, in large bowl, combine granulated sugar, baking powder, lemon juice, remaining flour and eggs. Mix well. Pour over baked crust and bake 20-25 minutes in 350° oven or until golden brown. Sprinkle with powdered sugar. Store in refrigerator.

ARKANSAS DIRT
1 12oz. carton Cool Whip
3 packages instant chocolate pudding
1 package Oreo cookies
8oz. cream cheese
3/4 stick margarine
1 cup powdered sugar
4 cups milk

Cream margarine and cream cheese. Add powdered sugar and cool whip. In separate bowl, mix pudding and milk. Add pudding to cream cheese mixture. In food processor or blender, grind cookies. In clean flower pot, put a layer of cookies and a layer of pudding. Keep layering until you end with cookies on top. This is fun to put in a flower pot and place an artificial flower in the middle and serve with a garden spade.

FRESH APPLE CAKE

2 cups sugar
1 cup oil
2 eggs
1 teaspoon cinnamon
1 teaspoon vanilla
1 teaspoon baking powder
1/2 teaspoon salt
2 cups fresh unpeeled apples, cored and diced
1 cup nuts
3 cups flour

Mix sugar, oil, eggs, cinnamon, vanilla, baking powder and salt, stirring with your hands. Add apples, flour, nuts and mix well. Pour batter into a well greased bundt pan and bake for 1 hour in a 350° oven.

PUMPKIN ICE CREAM PIE

1 quart vanilla ice cream, softened slightly
1 cup canned pumpkin
1/4 cup honey
2 1/2 teaspoon pumpkin pie spice
1 9 inch graham cracker pie shell
whipped cream
pecan halves to garnish

Working quickly, combine ice cream, pumpkin and honey with spices in a large bowl. Do not beat, but blend well. Pour mixture into pie shell and freeze immediately. Remove from freezer 15 minutes before serving. Garnish with whipped cream and pecans.

CHESS PIE
1 cup brown sugar
1/2 cup white sugar
1 teaspoon flour
1 teaspoon vanilla
1/2 cup butter, melted
2 tablespoon milk
2 eggs
1 9 inch pie shell, unbaked

Mix sugar and flour, add eggs to mixture. Add milk and vanilla. Mix in butter. Bake at 350° in unbaked pie shell for 40 minutes.

MANDARIN ORANGE FLUFF CAKE
1 yellow butter cake mix
4 eggs
1/2 cup oil
1 stick butter, melted
2 cans mandarin orange, drained

Mix well and pour into 2 prepared round cake pans. Bake at 350° until done.

FROSTING:
1 large can crushed pineapple
1 package instant vanilla pudding
1 large carton Cool Whip

Mix together and frost cake.

BOBBIE'S DUMP CAKE
1 box yellow cake mix
1 small package grated coconut
1 cup pecans
1 small can crushed pineapple
2 sticks butter

Pour 1 large can crushed pineapple into a 9 x 13 inch baking pan. Cover with 1 can shredded coconut. Take 1 yellow cake mix, dry and pour over the above. Sprinkle 1 cup of pecans on top of cake mix and lightly press them into mix. Cut 1 stick of butter into patties and place on top of mixture. Bake at 350° until done. Test with straw or toothpick until it comes out clean. Serve from the same pan.

AUNT BEA'S QUICK FRUIT PIE
1 can Eagle Brand milk
1 large can crushed pineapple
1/3 cup lemon juice
1/2 cup chopped pecans
1/2 cup coconut
1 carton cool whip
2 graham cracker pie shells

Mix all ingredients together well, except cool whip. Fold in cool whip. Pour in 2 graham cracker crusts and chill for 1 hour.

DERBY PIE

2 eggs
1 stick butter, melted
1 cup walnuts
1 cup chocolate chips
1/2 cup flour
1 cup sugar
1/2 teaspoon vanilla

Mix and pour into unbaked pie shell. Bake in 350 degree oven for 30-45 minutes.

THANKSGIVING & CHRISTMAS CHOCOLATE PIE

3 eggs, lightly beaten
1 cup white Karo syrup
1/2 cup white sugar
1/2 cup chocolate chips
2 tablespoon butter, melted
1 teaspoon vanilla
1 1/2 cups pecans
9" unbaked pie shell

Mix all ingredients in large bowl. Pour into a 9 inch unbaked pie shell. Bake in 350-degree oven 50-60 minutes or until inserted knife will come clean.

CHOCOLATE SOUFFLÉ

1/3 cup light cream
1 3oz. package cream cheese
1/2 cup semi-sweet chocolate chips
3 egg yolks
3 egg whites
1/4 cup powdered sugar

Preheat oven to 300°. In saucepan, blend cream and cream cheese over a low heat. Add chocolate chips, cook, stirring until melted, cool. Beat yolks with dash of salt until thick, about 5 minutes. Fold in egg whites. Blend to chocolate mixture, then fold into egg whites. Pour into buttered and sugared 1 quart soufflé dish and bake for 50 minutes. Sprinkle with powdered sugar and serve immediately with custard sauce.

CUSTARD SAUCE

4 egg yolks, beaten
dash of salt
1/4 cup sugar
2 cups milk, scalded
1 teaspoon vanilla

In saucepan, mix egg yolks, salt and sugar. Gradually add milk. Cook over low heat, stirring constantly until it coats silver spoon. Cool in cold water and add vanilla.

POUND CAKE

1 cup butter
1 cup milk
2 cups sugar
2 1/3 cups flour
5 eggs, separated
1/2 teaspoon salt
1/3 teaspoon baking powder

Mix all ingredients except salt and egg whites. Add salt to egg whites and beat. Fold egg whites into other ingredients. Bake 1 hour at 350 in greased tube pan.

IRON SKILLET CHOCOLATE PIE

1 cup sugar
2 tablespoon flour
2 tablespoon cocoa
2 tablespoon butter
3 egg yolks
1 cup milk
1 teaspoon vanilla
9 inch baked pie shell

Mix sugar, flour and cocoa in a mixing bowl and set aside. Melt butter in iron skillet and add sugar mixture. In separate bowl, beat egg yolks and milk. Add egg mixture to skillet a little at a time, stirring constantly. Cook slowly until thick. Remove from heat. Add vanilla and cool. Pour into baked pie shell.

RASPBERRY CHANTILLY

1 10oz. package frozen raspberries
1 tablespoon cornstarch
dash of salt
1/2 cup whipping cream
4 teaspoon sugar
1/2 cup sour cream
1/2 teaspoon vanilla

Thaw raspberries, drain and reserve syrup. Mix cornstarch, salt and syrup and cook until thick and clear. Fold in berries and cool. Beat cream, then add sugar. Fold in sour cream and vanilla. Put in sherbet glasses and swirl raspberry mixture over top before it sets. Can be served in parfait glasses in layers.

CHOCAROON CAKE

2 egg whites
1/3 cup sugar
2 tablespoon flour
1 3/4 cups coconut
1 chocolate cake mix
1 package instant chocolate pudding
2 egg yolks
1 1/2 cups water
1/3 cup oil

Beat egg whites until foamy. Add sugar and beat until stiff. Blend flour and coconut and set aside. Combine remaining ingredients in large bowl, blend 2 minutes. Pour 1/3 mix in bundt pan, spoon in coconut mixture and top with remaining mix. Bake 50-55 minutes at 350°.

CHESS CAKE
1 box yellow cake mix
2 whole eggs
1 stick melted margarine

Mix and pour into 9 x 13 inch baking pan.

1 box powdered sugar
1 stick melted margarine
2 whole eggs
1 package cream cheese

Beat all ingredients together and pour on top of cake mixture. Bake 50 minutes at 325°.

MINT DAZZLE DESSERT
1 cup butter, softened
3 cups powdered sugar
6 eggs, slightly beaten
6 squares unsweetened chocolate, melted
1 package miniature marshmallows
1/2 cup whipping cream
1/4 cup sugar
1/2 teaspoon vanilla
1/2 cup crushed peppermint stick candy

Cream together soft margarine, sugar, eggs and chocolate. Beat at high speed until very light and fluffy. Spoon over graham cracker crumbs. Put in freezer until firm. Mix whipping cream, sugar and vanilla together. Beat until soft peaks are formed. Fold in marshmallows. Spread over chocolate layer and sprinkle with candy. Wrap in plastic wrap tightly and freeze. Cut into small pieces since it is such a rich dessert. Set it out 15-20 minutes before serving. (continued on next page)

CRUST:
1/4 cup melted butter
1-2 tablespoons sugar
2 cups graham cracker crumbs

Bake at 350 for 10 minutes in 9 x 13 inch pan.

BUTTER CRUST
1 1/2 cups flour
1/2 cup margarine
2 tablespoon sour cream

Mix well and press into 9 inch pie pan. Bake 10 minutes or until golden brown, at 375°.

FRESH PEACH PIE
2 cups sliced peaches
1 tablespoon lemon juice
3 tablespoons cornstarch
3/4 cup sugar
2 teaspoon margarine
1/4 teaspoon almond extract
(1) 9 inch baked pie shell

Sprinkle peaches with lemon juice and sugar and let stand 1 hour. Drain and measure 1 cup syrup, add to cornstarch and blend. Stir over low heat until thick. Add margarine and extract and cool. Place peaches in baked pie shell and pour cool mixture over peaches. Serve with fresh, whipped cream and maraschino cherries.

WINTER FRUIT COMPOTE

3 medium grapefruits
1 cup sugar
1/2 cup marmalade
2 cups fresh cranberries
3 medium bananas

Peel and section grapefruit, reserving juice, set aside. Add enough water to juice to make 1 cup. Combine sugar and marmalade with juice. Heat to boiling, stirring to dissolve sugar. Add cranberries, cook and sir until they pop. Remove from heat and cool. Add grapefruit. Cover and chill. Just before serving, add sliced bananas to chilled mixture. Makes 10 servings.

SNOW PUDDING

1 tablespoon gelatin
1/4 cup cold water
2/3 cup boiling water
2/3 cup sugar
1/8 teaspoon salt
1/4 cup lemon juice
grated rind of 1 lemon
2 egg whites

Soak gelatin in cold water for about 5 minutes. Add boiling water to softened gelatin and stir until dissolved. Add sugar and stir to dissolve. Add salt, lemon juice and rind. Set bowl in refrigerator and chill until slightly thickened. Beat egg whites to stiff peaks. Beat thickened gelatin until foamy, add to egg whites and continue beating until mixture is fluffy. Place in refrigerator until firm. Spoon into sherbet glasses and top with chilled custard sauce.

LOIS' LEMON SUPREME SPECIAL
1 lemon cake mix
1/2 cup sugar
4 eggs
1 cup apricot nectar
1/2 cup Crisco oil

Blend all ingredients in large bowl. Beat at medium speed for 2 minutes. Spread batter in a greased and floured 10 inch tube pan. Bake at 250° for 45-55 minutes or until center springs back when touched lightly. Cool right side up for 15 minutes, then remove from pan.

GLAZE:
Blend 1 cup confectioner's sugar and 2 tablespoons lemon juice. Add a little milk. Pour over warm baked cake.

TEXAS SHEET CAKE
MIX:
2 cups sugar
2 cups flour
1/2 teaspoon salt

IN SAUCEPAN HEAT:
2 sticks butter
1 cup water
3 tablespoon cocoa
Pour over sugar mixture.

IN SEPARATE BOWL:
2 eggs
1 teaspoon soda
1/2 cup buttermilk
(continued on page 125)

1 teaspoon vanilla
1 teaspoon cinnamon

Mix and add to other mix. Grease and flour pan and bake at 350° for 20 minutes.

FROSTING:
1 stick butter, melted
3 tablespoon cocoa
6 tablespoon milk
1 box powdered sugar
1 teaspoon vanilla

Mix all ingredients 5 minutes before cake is done and pour over cake while it is hot. Add chopped pecans on top of frosting if desired.

$300 STRAWBERRY CAKE

1 box strawberry cake mix
1 box frozen sliced strawberries
1 box confectioners' sugar
1 medium container cool whip
1 pint fresh strawberries
1 8 oz. package cream cheese

Bake cake as directed on box. Allow to cool. Drain strawberries, punch holes in bottom layer of cake. Pour strawberry juice over cake. In large bowl, mix cream cheese and confectioners' sugar. Fold in strawberries. Frost cake and top with fresh strawberries.

GRANNY'S TEA CAKES
1 cup sugar
2 sticks margarine
1 teaspoon vanilla
1 egg
1/2 teaspoon soda
1/2 teaspoon salt
2 1/2 cups flour

Cream sugar, margarine, vanilla and egg. Add soda and salt. Blend in flour. Roll out dough and cut into cookies. Bake at 350° for 10-12 minutes.

MICROWAVE CHOCOLATE PIE
2 cups miniature marshmallows
1 cup milk chocolate chips
1 - 1oz. square unsweetened chocolate
1 cup whipping cream, whipped
1/2 cup milk
(1) 9 inch pie crust

Combine marshmallows, chocolate chips, milk and chocolate in 2 quart mixing bowl. Microwave 4-5 minutes, stirring once. Cool. Fold in whipping cream, pour into crust and freeze until firm.

SWEDISH PECAN BALLS

1 cup ground pecans
2 tablespoon sugar
1/2 cup butter
1 cup flour
1/8 teaspoon salt
1 teaspoon vanilla
1/2 cup powdered sugar

Combine all ingredients except powdered sugar and mix well. Shape dough into balls the size of walnuts. Place on ungreased cookie sheet and bake at 275° for about 30 minutes or until light brown. Roll in powdered sugar while hot and again after cookies have cooled.

BUCK EYES

1/2 bar paraffin
1 12 oz. package of chocolate chips
1 stick margarine
2 cups peanut butter
3 cups rice crispies
1 box powdered sugar

In double boiler, melt paraffin and chocolate chips. Mix together the remaining ingredients. Make 1 inch balls and dip in mixture. Set on wax paper and put in freezer for 10 minutes.

COLD BREAD PUDDING
8 leftover biscuits
1 cup sugar
1/2 to 3/4 cup milk
3 eggs
1 teaspoon vanilla

Crumble up biscuits in a bowl, add sugar and milk. Add eggs to the mixture and stir well. Stir in vanilla. Pour mixture into a greased and floured 9 inch cake pan and bake at 350° until done. Take from oven onto plate. Serve with pudding dip.

PUDDING DIP
2 cups milk
1 cup sugar
1 tablespoon cornstarch
1 teaspoon vanilla

Mix sugar and cornstarch, add milk slowly, stirring constantly. Add vanilla. Cook over medium heat, stirring constantly to prevent sticking. Thickens as it cools

CRISP OATMEAL COOKIES

1 cup brown sugar
1 cup white sugar
1 cup margarine
2 eggs
2 cups sifted flour
1 teaspoon soda
2 cups rice crispies
2 cups oats, uncooked
1 cup coconut
1 cup chopped nuts
1/2 cup raisins

Cream sugars, butter and eggs together. Mix all dry ingredients. Add remaining ingredients. Drop cookies on cookie sheet and bake at 350° for 8-10 minutes.

OLD FASHIONED BUTTERMILK PIE

1/4 cup butter, softened
2 cups sugar
3 eggs
1/4 cup flour
1 teaspoon vanilla
dash of nutmeg
1 unbaked 9 inch pie shell
1 cup buttermilk

Combine butter and sugar, creaming well. Add eggs and flour, beat until fluffy, about 2 minutes. Fold in buttermilk, vanilla and nutmeg. Pour filling into shell and bake at 350° for 50 minutes.

CHOCOLATE SYRUP BROWNIES

1/2 cup margarine
1 cup sugar
4 eggs
1 16oz. chocolate syrup
1 1/4 cup flour
1 cup nuts
quick chocolate glaze

In large mixing bowl, beat margarine on medium speed, add sugar, beat until fluffy. Add eggs and beat well. Stir in syrup and flour. Fold in nuts. Spread batter in greased 9 x 13 inch pan. Bake for 30 minutes at 350°.

GLAZE:
2/3 cup sugar
3 tablespoon milk
3 tablespoon margarine
2/3 cup semi-sweet chocolate chips

In saucepan, combine sugar, milk and margarine. Heat until boiling for 30 seconds. Stir in 2/3 cup semi-sweet chocolate chiips. Glaze warm brownies, enjoy!

SNOW ICE CREAM
Have ingredients on hand for when it snows!

1 can Eagle brand milk
4 eggs
1 cup sugar
2 tablespoon vanilla
3 cups milk

Mix well in blender until all sugar melts. Now-go get a huge pan of fluffy, clean snow. Add snow to the mixture until it is the consistency of ice cream and eat. Whatever you have left over, put in plastic cups in the freezer. This will be good all year. Be sure to hide yourself some.

SOUR CREAM POUND CAKE
2 sticks butter
3 cups sugar
6 eggs
1 cup sour cream
1/4 teaspoon soda
3 cups flour
1 teaspoon vanilla

Sift flour and soda. Cream butter and add sugar, beat well. Stir in sour cream, eggs, vanilla and gradually add flour. Use salt free shortening to grease pan. Bake in 325°oven for 1 1/2 hours. Let set in pan 5 minutes, before turning onto cake plate.

DOUBLE GOOD BROWNIES

1/2 cup butter
3 tablespoon cocoa
1 cup sugar
3/4 cup chopped nuts
2/3 cup self-rising flour
1 teaspoon vanilla
2 eggs

Heat oven to 350°. Melt butter and chocolate. Remove from heat and add all ingredients. Beat well. Pour into 8 1/2 x 9 inch pan. Bake for 30 minutes.

ICING:
2 tablespoon margarine
1 1/2 tablespoon cocoa
3 tablespoon hot water
2 1/2 cups powdered sugar
1 teaspoon vanilla
1 1/2 cups marshmallows

Melt margarine and cocoa. Add water, after blending margarine and cocoa, stir in sugar and vanilla. If necessary, add a little more water. Add marshmallows. Spread mixture over brownies. After spreading icing, place in broiler on medium and melt the marshmallows to spread evenly.

PEANUT BRITTLE

3 cups white sugar
1 cup Karo syrup
1/2 cup water
3 cups raw peanuts
3 teaspoon margarine
1 teaspoon salt
2 teaspoon soda

Bring everything to a boil except nuts. Add nuts and cook until nuts start to crack. Pour into pie tin and cool.

GRAPE ICE CREAM

4 eggs
4 cups sugar
1 tablespoon vanilla
dash of salt
1 pint whipping cream
5 cans grape soda

Cream eggs and sugar with electric mixer. Add whipping cream, vanilla and salt, to this add grape soda. Pour into 4-6 quart freezer tub, if not full add regular milk to fill. Freeze in electric or crank freezer.

MAGIC COOKIES

1/2 cup margarine
1 1/2 cup graham cracker crumbs
1 can Eagle Brand milk
1 package chocolate chips
3 1/2 oz. coconut
1 cup chopped nuts

Preheat oven to 350°. In 9 x 13 inch pan, melt margarine, sprinkle graham cracker crumbs over margarine. Layer chocolate chips, nuts and coconut. Pour Eagle Brand over evenly and bake 25-30 minutes. Do not over bake. Cool and cut into squares or bars. Store loosely covered. Do not refrigerate.

APPLE STRUDEL

1 1/2 cup chopped crisp apples
1/2 cup sugar
1/4 cup water
1/2 stick butter
1/2 teaspoon cinnamon

Line pan with apples. Sprinkle in sugar, water, butter and cinnamon.

CRUST:

1 cup flour, self-rising
1 cup sugar
1/2 cup shortening
1 egg

Mix well and spoon drop over apples. Bake in 350-degree oven to a golden brown. Serve with vanilla ice cream or whipped cream.

PINEAPPLE UPSIDE DOWN CAKE

1 1/2 stick margarine
1/2 box dark brown sugar
1 box yellow cake mix
Maraschino cherries
Pineapple rings

Melt the butter in iron skillet and add brown sugar. Add pineapple rings to cover bottom of skillet. Put cherries in the center of pineapple rings. Mix cake mix according to directions on box and pour into the skillet. Cook for approximately 40-45 minutes at 350°. Let cool 5 minutes and pour onto large plate.

COCONUT PIE

1 can Pet milk
6 tablespoon flour
1 1/2 cups water
1 1/4 cups sugar
3 egg yolks
3/4 stick butter
1 teaspoon vanilla
1/2 can coconut

Mix sugar and flour, add 1/4 cup of milk and egg yolks. Beat together well. Add remaining ingredients, except for last 3 ingredients. Cook over medium heat until thick. Remove from heat add last 3 ingredients. After the butter is melted and everything is blended well, pour into baked pie shell. Top with meringue, sprinkle with coconut and brown.

JAPANESE CHOCOLATE PIE

2 sticks margarine
1 1/2 cup chopped nuts
1 cup semi-sweet chocolate chips
4 eggs
1 cup coconut
2 unbaked pie shells

Melt chocolate and margarine over low heat. Stir until melted. Keep warm. Add other ingredients to melted chocolate. Pour into 2 unbaked pie shells. Bake at 325 for 35-40 minutes. Delicious served with vanilla ice cream.

FRESH COCONUT CAKE

~~2 cups whipping cream~~
1½ ~~2~~ cups sugar
½ 2 cups self-rising flour
4 eggs, separate and whipp the egg whites
1 teaspoon vanilla
milk from 1-2 coconuts — should equal 1 OR ½ C.

~~Whip cream,~~ add sugar and flour. Mix egg yolks and vanilla. ~~Fold in egg whites.~~ Pour into three 9 inch layer cake pans that are lightly greased and floured. Bake at 350° for ~~45~~ minutes. 25-30 min
After baked, poke holes in cake and pour coconut milk on cake. After cool, ice with recipe below.

(continued on next page)

USE 7 mi FROSTING FOR THIS CAKE (Pg 110) AFTER FROSTING CAKE - APPLY PLENTY OF COCONUT (FRESH FROZEN) ALSO PUT COCONUT BETWEEN LAYERS - AFTER CAKE IS FINISHED USE A THIN KNIFE BLADE TO POKE HOLES IN TOP OF CAKE & POUR IN COCONUT MILK PRESS CAKE BACK TOGATHER COVER & REFRIGERATE

FRESH COCONUT ICING:
2 unbeaten egg whites
1 1/2 cup sugar
6 tablespoon cold water
1/4 teaspoon cream of tartar
1 1/2 teaspoon light corn syrup
1 teaspoon vanilla

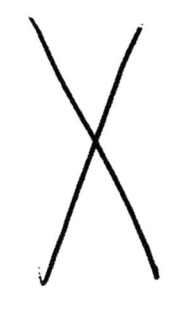

Place all ingredients in top of double boiler and beat until thoroughly blended. Place ingredients over rapidly boiling water. Beat 7 minutes. Remove from heat and add 1 teaspoon of vanilla. Ice cake and sprinkle with coconut. To save time, I use a cake mix and pour coconut milk over the cake and ice with this recipe.

CHOCOLATE PIE
3/4 can Hershey's syrup
1 can Pet milk
1 1/4 cups water
6 tablespoon flour
1 1/2 cups sugar
2 egg yolks
1 teaspoon vanilla
3/4 cup butter
1 Pet Ritz pie shell, baked

Mix sugar and flour. Add the syrup and the eggs. Blend well on low speed with the mixer. After it is blended well, add Pet milk and water and cook until thick on medium high (May need to cook on medium, depending on your stove). Remove from heat and add vanilla and butter. After butter melts, pour mixture into a cooked pie shell and add meringue topping.

TREASURE COOKIES

1 1/2 cup graham cracker crumbs
1/2 cup unsifted flour
2 teaspoon baking powder
14 oz. can Eagle Brand milk
1/2 cup margarine or butter, softened
1 1/3 cup flaked coconut
12 oz. semi-sweet chocolate chips
1 cup chopped walnuts or pecans

Preheat oven to 375°. In small bowl, mix graham cracker crumbs, flour and baking powder. In large mixer bowl, beat milk and margarine until smooth. Add graham cracker mixture and mix well. Stir in coconut, chocolate chips and nuts. Drop by rounded tablespoon on to ungreased cookie sheet. Bake 9-10 minutes. Store loosely covered at room temperature. Makes about 3 doz.en.

SOCK IT TO ME CAKE

1 package yellow cake mix, not butter
3/4 cup Crisco oil
1/2 cup sugar
2 teaspoon vanilla
4 eggs
8 oz. sour cream

Mix all ingredients and blend with electric mixer on medium speed. Pour into 9 x 13 pan or tube pan, well greased.

(continued on next page)

SOCK IT TO ME CAKE TOPPING:
Mix 2 teaspoons cinnamon, 3 tablespoons light brown sugar and 1/2 cup chopped pecans. Mix well and spoon on top of batter. Cut into batter with a knife. Bake for 30-40 minutes at 350°.

GLAZE FOR SOCK IT TO ME CAKE
2 tablespoon margarine
2 tablespoon milk
1 cup sifted powdered sugar
1 teaspoon vanilla

Mix all ingredients together well. Spoon glaze on top of cooked cake while hot. Enjoy!

BRITTNEY COOKIES
Leftover pie doe. Roll out oblong and thin. Place in pie Pyrex 9 x 13 dish. Sprinkle half of doe with 1ST FILLING: Brown shurger to cover well. Dot with pats of butter. Sprinkle with cinammin. 2ND FILLING: 1/3 cup of white shurger, mix well with one tablespoon of choccklete. Dot with pats of butter. Fold uncovered half of crust over covered filling. Place in oven at 400° until brown. (This recipe was submitted as is by Brittney Byerley, Vestal's 8 year old granddaughter).

CHOCOLATE GRAVY

2 tablespoon cocoa
1 1/2 cups sugar
2 tablespoon all purpose flour
1 teaspoon vanilla extract
3 cups water

In a saucepan, combine the cocoa, sugar, flour, vanilla and water. Cook over medium heat until it boils. The mixture will slowly thicken. Cook for about 10 minutes. Pour over buttered hot biscuits.

CHERRY CHEESE PIE

1 graham cracker pie shell
8 oz. cream cheese
1 can Eagle Brand milk
1/2 cup lemon juice
1 teaspoon vanilla
1 can cherry pie filling

Beat together cream cheese and milk. Stir in lemon juice and vanilla. Pour in pie shell. Chill 2 hours. Top with cherry pie filling.

CHOCOLATE COVERED BALLS

1 stick margarine, room temperature
1 small can Carnation milk
2 boxes confectioners' sugar
12 oz. jar crunchy peanut butter

Mix well using can milk to get consistency desired to form ball. Let stand in refrigerator for about 2 hours until firm. Melt 2 ounces paraffin wax, (1/2 stick) and 12 ounces chocolate chips in a double boiler. Stick peanut butter balls with a toothpick and dip in chocolate mixture, and place on wax paper.

SPECIAL MIXING INSTRUCTIONS: *Mix sugar with room temperature margarine, pouring milk slowly. Then add extra ingredients, either peanut butter, pecan chips or coconut. If using cherries, be sure they are candied and place them in last. MUST refrigerate before dipping.*

Vestal & Friends

GEORGE JONES' SPICY THREE BEAN SOUP

3 chicken breasts
3 cups water
2 (28oz.) cans chopped tomatoes
1 (10oz.) package frozen cut green beans
1 (10oz.) package frozen baby green lima beans
2 bay leaves
2 tablespoon Creole seasoning
1 teaspoon chili powder
1 teaspoon paprika
1/4 teaspoon garlic powder
1/4 to 1/2 teaspoon cayenne pepper
dash of Tabasco sauce
dash of soy sauce
dash of Worcestershire sauce
1 (15oz.) can black beans, drained

Combine all ingredients, except black beans, in a large stockpot. Bring to a boil, reduce heat. Simmer covered for 1 hour. Remove chicken from soup. Let cool. Debone chicken and chop into pieces. Return chicken to soup. Stir in black beans. Cook until heated through. Remove bay leaves. May add 1/2 small box cooked macaroni when adding black beans.

JANET PASCHAL'S LEMON PIE

1 baked 9 inch pie shell
1 1/4 cup sugar
6 tablespoon cornstarch
2 cups water
1/3 cup lemon juice
3 egg yolks
1 1/2 teaspoon lemon extract
2 teaspoon vinegar
3 tablespoon butter

Mix sugar and cornstarch together in the top of double boiler. Add 2 cups water. Combine egg yolks with lemon juice and beat until well mixed. Add to the rest of the sugar mixture. Cook over boiling water until thick, about 25 minutes. This eliminates the starchy taste. Now, add the lemon extract, butter, vinegar and stir thoroughly. Pour mixture into pie shell and let cool. Cover with Never Fail Meringue and brown.
(see Janet's Never Fail Meringue recipe on next page)

NEVER FAIL MERINGUE
1 tablespoon cornstarch
2 tablespoon cold water
1/4 cup boiling water
3 egg whites
6 teaspoon sugar
1 teaspoon vanilla
pinch of salt

Blend cornstarch and cold water in a saucepan. Add boiling water and cook, stirring until clear and thickened. Let stand until completely cold. With electric beater at high speed, beat egg whites until foamy. Gradually add sugar and beat until stiff but not dry. Turn mixer to low speed and add salt and vanilla. Gradually beat in cold cornstarch mixture. Turn mixer again to high and beat well. Spread meringue over cooled pie filling. Bake at 350° for 10 minutes, or until top is lightly browned.

GLORIA GAITHER'S WHEAT BREAD

IN A LARGE BOWL:
1/2 cup warm water
1 teaspoon sugar
1 package dry yeast
1/8 teaspoon ginger

ADD:
2 teaspoon vegetable oil
2 teaspoon honey
1 15oz. can condensed milk

Mix the above items together, then add the following. Mix mostly with electric mixer. Mix the final cup of flour by hand.

MIX:
1 cup whole wheat flour
3 cup unbleached white flour

Drop the batter in two 1 pound or on 2 pound coffee cans, well greased. Grease plastic lid and seal cans. Let rise until lids pop off. Bake at 330-350° for about 30-40 minutes or until golden brown. Let cool slightly before removing from cans. Serve hot.

NEWSBOYS AUSTRALIAN SUNDAY LUNCH ROASTED LEG OF LAMB

1 medium leg of lamb
6 small potatoes
10 baby carrots
1 medium sized onion, cut up
salt and pepper to taste
fresh rosemary sprigs
olive oil

Sprinkle olive oil on lamb. Put lamb in oven bag with salt, pepper and rosemary. Cook 1 1/2 hours at 325°. Place vegetables outside of bag on tray and cook another 30 minutes. Serve with mint jelly. English peas are always a great side dish.

VINCE GILL'S FAVORITE RECIPE
Domino's
Pizza Hut Delivery
Papa John's Pizza
Little Caesar's Pizza

Pick a pizza delivery, call their number and order your favorite pizza. Sit back and wait for your order to arrive. Enjoy!

KATINA'S FRUIT PIZZA

CRUST:
1 cup flour
1/4 cup powdered sugar
1/2 cup melted butter

FILLING:
8 oz. softened cream cheese
1 teaspoon vanilla
1/3 cup sugar

GLAZE:
1 cup pineapple juice
2 tablespoon cornstarch
1/3 cup sugar
1 teaspoon lemon juice
boil and set aside

Combine crust ingredients and form into a ball. Spread onto a round pizza pan. Bake at 350° for 8-10 minutes. Cool and spread with filling. Cover with fruit in a circular design. Cover with glaze. Refrigerate for at least 2 hours. Cut like a pizza and serve.

ISLANDS IN THE STREAM
BY DOLLY PARTON

3 eggs, separated
2/3 cup sugar
2 heaping teaspoons flour
1 quart milk
1 teaspoon vanilla
nutmeg, optional

Cream egg yolks with sugar. Whip until smooth. Add flour. Mix well. Scald milk and immediately add to cream mixture. Cook for 20-25 minutes, stirring constantly, until mixture thickens. Remove from heat and add vanilla. In a separate bowl, whip egg whites. Bring a pot of water to boiling stage. Add egg whites to the boiling water until hardened. Remove egg whites with a spatula and put on top of cream mixture. Sprinkle with nutmeg if desired. Chill for at least 1 hour, then serve.

JAKE HESS' ORANGE JELL-O SALAD

1 can mandarin oranges
1 small can crushed pineapple
1 tablespoon sugar
1 large package orange Jell-O
12 large marshmallows
3oz. package cream cheese
1/2 pint whipping cream

Drain juice from fruit and add enough water to make 2 cups of liquid. Add 1 tablespoon sugar and bring to a boil. Add Jell-O, dissolve and add marshmallows. Cut up and stir in cream cheese. Cool quickly and refrigerate until slightly thickened. Add pineapple, oranges and whipped cream. The whipping cream should be whipped to a thick firm texture before adding to mixture. Return to refrigerator until firm.

RUSS TAFF'S CHILI DOGS

1 lb ground beef
3 tablespoon chili powder
1 can tomato sauce
1 can tomato soup
2 cups water
1 can ranch style beans
1 small onion, minced
1 tablespoon cumin
1 teaspoon minced garlic
1 small jalepeno, minced
1 package beef wieners
1 package hot dog buns

In skillet, brown ground beef. In large stockpot, combine chili powder, tomato sauce, soup and water and bring to a boil. Chop onion in small pieces. Place half of onion in the sauce mixture along with beans. When at full boil, add beef, cumin, garlic and minced jalepeno to taste. Simmer on low for 1 hour. Boil hotdogs and pour chili over hot dogs and buns. Use reserved onion at your own risk.

SANDI PATTY'S MOST SPECTACULAR MEATLOAF

3 lbs extra lean ground beef
1 small box Grapenuts cereal
1/2 cup diced onion
pepper and garlic powder to taste
2 eggs, beaten

Mix the above ingredients together

1 cup catsup
1 cup light waffle syrup
2 tablespoon mustard

In separate bowl, mix the above ingredients for glaze. Poke holes in meat and pour glaze over meat. Bake at 350° for 1 1/2 - 2 hours until it is really brown around the edges. Let sit for 20-30 minutes prior to serving.

ANDRAE CROUCH'S FRIED CHICKEN

1 fryer, cut up
2 1/2 cups flour
1 tablespoon salt
2 tablespoon black pepper
2 tablespoon Lawry's seasoning salt
2 tablespoon paprika
1 brown paper bag

In brown paper bag, combine flour, salts, pepper and paprika. Shake bag to mix. Taste flour for saltiness. Heat grease until bubbly and lower heat. Place a few pieces of chicken in bag and shake until all pieces are well covered, repeat for all pieces of chicken. Place chicken in pan and fry until done. Drain chicken on paper towel.

CARMAN'S FAVORITE SPAGHETTI SAUCE AND MEATBALLS

As made by his mother, Nancy Licciardello. This recipe is very old, it was originally Mrs.Licciardello's great grandmother's. A few revisions have been made over the years.

1 package beef neckbones 1 1/2 lbs **
1 package pork neckbones 1 1/2 lbs **
6 links of Italian sausage
1/4 teaspoon fennel seasoning
1 teaspoon oregano
1 medium onion
1 cup olive oil
1 tablespoon salt
1 tablespoon sugar
1 teaspoon black pepper
6 large cloves of fresh garlic, chopped
1 large jar Ragu sauce with mushrooms
1 large can Hunt's tomato sauce (15 1/2 oz.)
4 large basil leaves
**If no neckbones are available, use pieces of beef and pork.

Brown pork, beef and cut up pieces of sausage with all the seasonings, in olive in a large 8 quart cooking pot. Add garlic, onion and basil. Brown lightly. Add the tomato sauce with 1/2 can of water for every can of sauce. Add tomato paste and one can of water to pot. Allow sauce to come to a boil, stirring occasionally, then lower heat, sprinkle in some sugar and continue simmering. Taste sauce at this point to make sure there is enough sugar and salt for your liking.

INGREDIENTS FOR MEATBALLS

2 lbs ground meat (beef, pork & veal)
6 large leaves of fresh basil, cut up
1/2 cup fresh parsley, cut up
4 extra large eggs
3/4 cup milk
1/2 cup Italian grated cheese
3/4 cup Italian breadcrumbs
1/4 cup water
4 large cloves of fresh garlic, chopped
1 medium onion, chopped
1 teaspoon salt
1 teaspoon black pepper

To a large mixing bowl, add ground meat, eggs, cheese, parsley, basil and garlic, salt, black pepper, milk and water. Add bread crumbs to hold other ingredients together before shaping balls. Mix well and form into meatballs, a little larger than golf ball size. Brown meatballs in large frying pan with oil. After meatballs are browned, toss them into sauce with remaining oil. Add a little water to emptied frying pan and add to sauce, to gather all of the flavor. Allow sauce to cook on medium low heat for 2 1/2 - 3 hours, stirring occasionally so as not to burn. Cook sauce until meat pieces are tender and soft. Prepare spaghetti when sauce is cooked. Add spaghetti, or any other type of macaroni to 6-8 quart pot of boiling water. Stir to avoid sticking together. Angel hair only requires 5-6 minutes. Drain in colander. Place strained macaroni in large bowl, already lined with sauce. Add more sauce, along with some grated cheese, mix spaghetti to absorb the sauce. Add more sauce to top of spaghetti. Have extra sauce in serving pitcher to allow each guest more sauce as desired. Spaghetti should always be served hot, as it cools down rapidly. Serve meatballs and other meats on the side.

www.VestalandFriends.com

For More Information On the Music, Video's & Product Available By:

Vestal and The Happy Goodman's

Vestal & Friends CD
Vol. 1 & 2

Featuring Duets with George Jones, Dolly Parton, Bill & Gloria Gaither, Vince Gill, Wynonna and many more...

Call
800-717-7773

(All Major Credit Cards Accepted)

or write to:

GOODMAN FAMILY MINISTRIES
P.O. BOX 158778
NASHVILLE, TN. 37215

COOKBOOK 2
Second Helpings
Now Available!

www.VestalandFriends.com